D1358130

Divorce and Your Child

Divorce and Your Child

Practical Suggestions for Parents

**Sonja Goldstein, LL.B., and
Albert J. Solnit, M.D.**

Yale University Press
New Haven and London

Designed by James J. Johnson
and set in Times Roman type.
Printed in the United States of America by
Vail-Ballou Press, Binghamton, New York.

Library of Congress Cataloging in Publication Data

Goldstein, Sonja, 1926–
    Divorce and your child.

    Bibliography: p.
    Includes index.
    1. Children of divorced parents—United States.
    2. Child development—United States. 3. Child
Custody—United States. I. Solnit, Albert J. II. Title.
HQ777.5.G64 1984   646.7'8   83–51297
ISBN 0–300–02810–5
        0–300–03414–8 (pbk.)

*The paper in this book meets the guidelines for perma-
nence and durability of the Committee on Production
Guidelines for Book Longevity of the Council on Library
Resources.*

10   9   8   7   6   5   4   3

For Our Families

Contents

Acknowledgments

This book has been shaped by family, friends, colleagues, clients, and patients. We acknowledge our appreciation to all of them.

Our special thanks go to Joseph Goldstein, for his substantive and editorial contributions, detailed reading and critique, and, above all, unfailing support; Joshua Goldstein, for his unflinching criticism and constructive suggestions; Anne Goldstein, for her early reading of our manuscript and her encouragement; Gladys Topkis, for her kind but firm and demanding editing; Elizabeth Sharp, for her generous, loyal, and beyond-the-call-of-duty assistance; and Dolores Gee, Rosemarie Willis, and Lisa Carpentino, for their cheerful and competent typing.

We are grateful to the late Anna Freud for her lively interest in our work and for her valuable suggestions.

1

Introduction

If we were living in a world governed by children's wishes, parents would rarely separate, no matter how badly they got along with each other. Children—and not only very young ones—need and rely on their mothers and fathers and tend to think of them as having no purpose in life other than to be their parents. They find it hard to understand and accept that their mother or father can actually move out of the home and, as they see it, abandon them.

Yet divorce and the separation of unmarried parents are commonplace. In the United States today almost 40 percent of all marriages end in divorce, affecting more than one million children each year and a total of twelve million children under the age of eighteen.[1] To this number must be added the children of unmarried parents who separate, for when a parent moves out of the home, the emotional impact on the child does not depend on the presence of a marriage certificate or divorce decree. Our laws and customs have made it increasingly easy for couples to dissolve their marriages and other significant relationships so that they may arrange their lives as they see fit. From the unhappy parents' point of view, separation is often a desirable step—indeed, sometimes the only possible solution to an intolerable situation. Even if such parents believe that their children would be better off if they remained together, they may feel it necessary and justifiable to put their own needs and interests first. But in fact many parents believe that their separation will improve their children's lives as well as their own. Either intuitively or in a reasoned way, they have reached the conclusion that whether the domestic conflicts have been quiet or noisy, violent or nonviolent, the cost to the children of their remaining together is greater than that of separation or divorce.

This is a book *for* separating parents. It is *about* children and their needs. We look at separation and divorce—the attitudes and actions of parents; the impact of laws and customs; the parts played in this often lengthy drama by parents, lawyers, psychologists, judges, psychiatrists, social workers, and other adults; the formation of new relationships—as they are perceived and experienced *by children.* One of us is a lawyer; the other a child psychiatrist and psychoanalyst. But this book is not a survey or an analysis of divorce laws, though it discusses the implications of laws for children's well-being. Nor does it assume that children of divorced parents necessarily have emotional problems that require professional treatment,[2] though it emphasizes the psychological impact of separation and divorce. Rather, we have translated our training and experience in law and child development—and as parents—into practical suggestions for parents who want to mitigate the impact of unsettling changes on their children's lives and, if possible, to turn them to constructive use. Our observations, except when related to legal consequences, are pertinent for separating parents whether or not they have been legally married to each other and whether or not their parting is legally sanctioned by a divorce decree.

We recognize that no two divorces are alike, because no two families are alike, and that every situation is special for members of that family. But because the parent-child relationship meets universal needs, you, the separating parents, are likely to confront situations that are not unique to you. Some of these are reflected in the following questions:

My husband and I are not happy together, and I'm sure my children are aware of this. I've read that so-called emotional divorce of the parents is worse for children than actual divorce. But I know many divorced women who seem to me to be more unhappy than before their divorces. Should I get a divorce for the sake of my children? (See chapter 3.)

I have been divorced for two years. As yet, I have not remarried. I know that my ten-year-old daughter secretly hopes that her father and I will one day get together again. This will never happen. Is it bad for her to have these fantasies, and should I make a point of trying to talk her out of them? (See chapter 3.)

My husband wants custody of our two preschool children—a boy and a girl. I don't want to let him have custody because he has left me to live with his girlfriend, and I don't see why he should have his cake and eat it too. On the other hand, the children would really hamper my career and social life. I feel very guilty about having this thought. My parents and all my friends take it for granted that I want to keep my children with me. What should I do? (See chapter 5.)

I can't imagine not having my children live with me, and I think I can do a better job bringing them up than my wife can, even though right now she is the one who is mostly taking care of them. Should I fight her for custody? If I don't, when my children grow older, will they blame me for having given them up? (See chapter 5.)

Whenever I hear a child expert on television describing maternal feelings, I don't think I have the right emotions. For instance, though I love my children, I always want to keep the best piece of meat for myself at dinner. Also, I'm bored spending all day with my preschooler. I just don't like playing with blocks. I'm getting divorced, and my husband wants custody. But I can't imagine life without my children. Is it all right for me to tell my lawyer I want custody, or am I bad for them? (See chapter 5.)

My ex-wife and I had a big legal battle about my having the children every other weekend. I finally won. I've tried taking them on outings. I've tried to share my interests with them, as the child guidance books say, but nothing works. When I fix the car I don't want to be teaching my six-year-old daughter how to do it. I don't like Walt Disney movies, and I hate popcorn. But I love my children. Should I spend my Sundays doing what I want or what they want? (See chapter 10.)

When I tell my lawyer that I ought to have custody of the children because my wife has lots of different boyfriends who come to the house, he says that children need their mother and that her morals have nothing to do with her fitness to be a mother. Should I go to another lawyer? Isn't my lawyer supposed to do what I tell him to do? (See chapter 6.)

Should I tell my children that our divorce is their father's fault because he is a no-good s.o.b. (which he is), or should I tell them that there are always two sides to a story and that divorce is nobody's fault, even though I don't really believe that? (See chapter 4.)

I always tell my children that their mother is a good person. But I know that when they are with her she tells them that I am a tyrant who made her life miserable and that the best thing she ever did was to get rid of me. Is this fair? (P.S. I hate her guts.) (See chapter 9.)

My teenage children live with me but spend very little time with me. I think they are selfish. When they were little I sacrificed a great deal for their sake. I stayed at home instead of going out on dates after my divorce. Don't they owe me something? (See chapter 9.)

My ex-husband has visitation rights every weekend and one month every summer. My ten-year-old daughter looks forward to these occasions, but my six-year-old boy dreads them. Should I encourage, urge, or force my son to go? He will do what I say. (See chapter 9.)

My wife and I have decided to get a divorce. We want to do what is right for our children—a boy of three, a boy of five, and a girl of eight. Should we ask each of them which of us they would rather live with? (See chapters 5 and 7.)

Some of the divorce books I've read say that when parents get divorced children think somehow it's their fault and that they should be told this is not so, that the divorce had nothing to do with them and did not happen because they were bad. So that's what I said to my ten-year-old daughter when my wife and I were getting a divorce. She looked at me and said, "Gee, it never occurred to me to think I was to blame." Do you think maybe I gave her ideas? (See chapter 4.)

I love my three-year-old son very much. Before my divorce he was very affectionate, and when he woke up during the night he always called to me for comfort. He lives with me, but now when I go near him he often says, "I hate you." I don't understand this and I don't know what to do. It makes me very angry as well as unhappy, even though I pretend I don't care and try to reassure him by telling him it's perfectly okay for him to hate me and that I love him anyway. Does this mean he would be better off if his mother had custody of him instead of me? (See chapters 3 and 9).

My ex-wife has recently remarried. She has custody of our two children, but I have been seeing them regularly with no problems. Now it seems that every time I want to take them out there is some excuse for them not coming. I think their stepfather is trying to win them away from me. Furthermore, he is a religious person and the whole family goes to worship every week. I'm an atheist and don't want my children to become seduced by religion. Should I try to get custody? (See chapter 12.)

Answers to these and other questions you may face must come from you, the parents, in terms of how you see your children's needs and how far you can comfortably meet them, for no one else lives inside your skin. Indeed, perhaps you cannot always think of your children first and foremost. The ending of your marriage is a difficult time. It may be for you a little like the death of your spouse and for your children like the death of a parent. Like death it does not end the relationship, except possibly in the physical sense; rather, it means calling up memories and seeing past events in a new light. And, like death, it may call forth a succession or combination of feelings such as shock, loss, helplessness, anger, rage, depression, and finally acceptance. You will probably feel lonely and isolated even if your decision to separate has brought a measure of relief to you and a relaxation of tension for your child. Your loneliness might be exacerbated if you have, in addition, lost the affection and companionship of your in-laws or even of your own family. Also, some friends may have dropped away instead of providing comfort and support, because they side with your spouse, because they disapprove of your chosen way of life, because they prefer not to have contact with either spouse so as not to be seen as taking sides, or because your anger and unhappiness make them uncomfortable. It may be hard for you to be as sensitive and responsive to your children as you would like to be while you as well as they are experiencing such emotions. The last thing you deserve is to be scolded by some "expert" and told that you are not doing right by your children. But you are faced with countless decisions, both large and small, before, during, and after your separation and divorce. You may receive advice, suggestions (solicited[3] or otherwise) and even orders from many sources—much of it conflicting and bewildering. It may not be at all clear whether the advice focuses on the interests of children, the family, or the parents or reflects some personal preference of the advice giver. If you don't know how your actions or behavior are likely to affect your children, you may make choices that you would not have made had you been better informed. It is in order to give some guidance to you, the mother and father who want to do the best you can to enhance your children's well-being, that we look at separation and divorce and their aftermath from a child's perspective.

Growing up is not a smooth process for any child. It is inevitably accompanied by inner—and often outer—turmoil. Your separation complicates this process for your children no matter how much you would like to spare them pain. They are bound to be affected by your separation whether it is gradual or sudden, amicable or bitter, and whether as a result of it they become estranged from one of you or not, though all these factors influence the extent and nature of the impact.[4] This is more easily understood when it is seen in the context of what an intact family means in the life of a child and how he[5] experiences its disruption. That is the subject of part I. In part II we look at the actual divorce process. Living with the divorce and establishing new family relationships are discussed in part III. Our emphasis throughout is on ways in which you, the parents, can help your children to meet and overcome the difficulties caused by your separation and divorce.

At one time we thought we might call this book "Divorce Family Style." We did not do so lest our readers think us facetious about important matters. Nonetheless, that title does convey what this book is about—children benefit when adults treat divorce as a family affair.

PART I.
Child Development and Family Life

2

Children and Their Families

Children are not miniature grown-ups. Though the healthy infant carries within himself the potential to become a healthy adult, this potential cannot be realized without the help of other factors that are not innate but environmental. Babies need constant physical care if they are to survive and grow. And because a child is a human being and not a machine, to ensure that he will thrive, he must be given physical care by an adult who has emotional ties to him.

The child's body needs to be tended, nourished and protected. His intellect needs to be stimulated and alerted to the happenings in his environment. He needs help in understanding and organizing his sensations and perceptions. He needs people to love, receive affection from, and to serve as safe targets for his infantile anger and aggression. He needs assistance from adults in modifying his primitive drives (sex and aggression). He needs patterns for identification provided by the parents to build up a functioning moral conscience. As much as anything else, he needs to be accepted, valued and wanted as a member of the family unit consisting of adults as well as other children. . . .

The parent who feeds the infant and puts him to bed thereby introduces a first compliance with a time schedule; the parents who grant but also withhold bodily and mental satisfactions help the child to realize that not all wishes can be fulfilled at all times. This increases the child's capacity to tolerate postponement of gratification and inevitable frustration.

The parents by reacting to the child's behavior with appropriate praise and encouragement, or criticism and discouragement, may lay the first foundations for the child's own control of his drives and impulses, the lessening of his selfishness, and the beginning of consideration for others.

The parents present a set of demands and prohibitions and attitudes toward work and community with which the child can identify.

Experiences with other children in the family strengthen these capacities, enable the child to gain a sense of community and provide additional opportunities for the child to form his conceptions of sharing, fair play and justice.[1]

As the child grows up, the family provides a safe setting in which he can take the many steps toward physical and emotional maturity. When he falters and falls in his first steps, he will be picked up, comforted, and encouraged to try again. When he does not succeed in building a tower of blocks or in making friends, he will be comforted, loved, cajoled, and encouraged to try again. When he fails to do his homework, stays out late, or is rude to parents or teachers, he will be scolded, cajoled, and loved into mending his ways. In adolescence the family provides a place of safety to which he can retreat from time to time, a place where he is accepted for what he is and where he can take a step or two backward when he has gone forward too fast for his inner time-table. Above all, his parents provide continuing love and nourishment for the self-esteem he needs to become a mature adult.

This picture of the family is, of course, highly idealized and, indeed, for some families completely false. Parents carry their own freight of problems and concerns and neither will nor always can provide adequate care and the proper mixture of love, discipline, and freedom the child needs. And the child's response to the love he receives or to the demands made on him may be disappointing to the parents and in turn may affect their future response to him. Yet in spite of its imperfections, the "family," however defined at different times and in different cultures, is the unit that has generally best provided the environment children need for healthy growth and development. Children who are shifted from foster home to foster home or who are brought up in institutions where they are unable to have long-term relationships with the adults who look after them are at a disadvantage. They may eventually become unable to form close relationships at any time in their lives.[2] Though the place of men and women in our society has been changing—more rapidly, perhaps, than ever before—there has been and will be no change in the basic need of children, from infancy to the teens, for continuity of care from at least one loving adult.

Our laws and social institutions generally reflect the recognition that, in spite of their inevitable shortcomings, most parents provide better opportunities for their children to thrive and grow up into reasonably healthy adults than any alternative our society has to offer. Unless they abandon or severely neglect or abuse their children, parents are basically left to bring them up as they see fit. "Freedom of personal choice in matters of . . . family life" is one of the liberties protected by the Due Process Clause of the Fourteenth Amendment.[3] Parents provide day-to-day care for children and make the major decisions affecting their lives. Community and government are intended mainly to be benevolent onlookers whose role is to provide schools, hospitals, recreational facilities, and services such as financial assistance and protection for neglected and abused children. This hands-off attitude, in turn, reinforces children's feelings of security—their parents will look after them and no outsider can interfere.

But when parents decide to divorce, the picture changes. When parents are in disagreement, outsiders may begin to intrude into their children's lives. Often divorce opens the door for lawyers, judges, social workers and other officials to have a say in who should care for the children and how they should do it. A judge may decide whether a child is to live with his mother or his father or part of the time with each; whether the parent with whom the child lives has the right to move with him to another town, state, or country; whether and when the other parent has the right to see the child; and whether the child will continue to live with his brothers and sisters or be separated from them.

Fortunately, in spite of the multitude of laws, rules, regulations, government officials, and child experts who may have a say in your divorce, you can influence custody decisions and thus retain greater control over your own life and your child's by the way in which you go about your divorce. Because all children need parents and therefore to some extent experience a common upheaval when their parents separate, we can make some generally applicable observations about the impact of divorce on children. These in turn will lead to some suggestions on how you can cushion your child against the adverse impact of your divorce and help him to live with the inevitable changes in his life.

3

Separation and Divorce from a Child's Perspective

The inner life of a child is intertwined with his physical growth and external circumstances. A baby's emotional need for his mother and father is grounded in his inability to take care of his own physical needs; at the same time, he may not thrive physically if he has no emotional attachment to his caregiving parents.[1] The separation of his parents affects the child's resolution of normal developmental conflicts. At the same time, his age and maturity influence the way in which he experiences this event. His reactions will also depend on his innate strengths and vulnerabilities and on family relationships before and after the separation.

Depending on the circumstances, a child may experience the separation of his parents not as a single event but as a series of changes, either abrupt or gradual, which may continue for a long time. In this and the following chapters we discuss two frequently overlapping phases in the preliminary stages of divorce. The first is parental conflict and estrangement; the second is separation and its immediate aftermath.

Before the Separation

Long before parents actually separate a child may sense that all is not well. There may be frequent quarrels of varying degrees of intensity and violence, prolonged silences, sulking, crying spells, or outbursts of temper by one or both parents, stilted conversations, and other signs of tension. A gulf of silence may develop between mother and father over time as they lead increasingly separate lives.

When there are loud quarrels or physical violence parental conflict is obvious. But even if these are not present, and even if the child is not told anything, he is likely to know that something is wrong. Whatever his age, he will feel anxious when there are continual tensions in the home, whether or not he understands the reasons for them. If the conflict between mother and father has been going on for a long time, there may not even be a change in the atmosphere; the child may never have known a family environment in which his parents were not fighting and pulling in different directions. Adults may think that because they say nothing about marital turmoil, because they shed their tears in private and carry out their quarrels behind closed doors, the child will not know something is wrong. But this is probably not so. Just as a child feels safe and protected in a home of loving, united parents without needing to be told, words are not necessary to make him feel insecure when he is living in the midst of parental tensions. Breastfeeding mothers sometimes notice that their milk does not flow as freely when they are upset as when they feel calm and peaceful. Mothers and fathers often find that when they are worried or unhappy they are not as successful in soothing a fretful child as at other times. Somehow or other, even when they try very hard to hide their feelings, parents and children communicate significantly with each other without words. And when tension and unhappiness are being resolved in the direction of separation and divorce, it is virtually certain that a child, whatever his age and however familiar he is with such tension, will become apprehensive that something is "wrong" and fearful that upsetting changes are about to take place.

When One Parent Moves Out

For a child who has been accustomed to both parents living at home and spending time with him, their actual separation represents a drastic change. No matter how strained the atmosphere was before, two parents lived in the home with him then, and now there is only one. The child's awareness that one parent has moved out for good may come gradually. Even though he may have been told that the separation is permanent, he may not absorb the fact for a while, perhaps because it is so painful that he denies it to himself. And if he has not been told what is going on, he may at first experience his father's absence, for instance, as no different from earlier absences on business trips or visits to relatives or friends. If his mother has stormed out of the house on previous occasions only to return a few days later, it may be a while before he realizes that this time she is not going to come back.

Once a child does realize that his mother or father has left home for good, unless the departing parent took no part at all in family life he will experience upsetting and painful emotions. Even though the lessening of conflict or tension may bring badly needed relief, he may feel puzzled, confused, and frightened because his sense of security, which was based on living with both parents, has been shaken.

Infants and Preschoolers

No matter how old the child is, he will wonder what will happen next. If he is under the age of seven or eight he may feel especially helpless. He may not see his parents' separation, as they do, as a necessary step to alleviate their unhappiness and promote everyone's welfare. He may not have the capacity to understand why his mother or father has moved out, and he may fear that he himself will be sent away or abandoned. What was beyond the realm of his comprehension before the separation—the departure of a parent—has now happened. How is he to know that it will not happen again?

If the child is an infant or toddler his fear of separation or abandonment can be pervasive, though nameless. The school-age child may fear, quite literally, that he will be deprived of the shelter, food, and other physical care which he is old enough to know he needs and is unable to furnish for himself. Even if he does not specifically fear being abandoned by the other parent as well, he may be afraid that further bad things will happen. Once his sense of security is shaken it cannot easily be restored, any more than a person who has once suffered a serious illness can quickly regain confidence in his invincible good health. And what parents may consider his unrealistic preoccupation with shelter, food, and clothing may be the child's way of expressing his deeply felt longing for affection and security.

Older Children

The adolescent is less dependent on his parents for actual physical care but usually continues to depend on them financially and emotionally. The teenager's assertiveness or rebellion may be a step in the process of separating from his parents in order to become an adult himself. Parents may often have felt that their teenager would like nothing better than to be free of their control. But he may be hampered in taking the necessary, though sometimes annoying, steps toward true adult independence if the demand for separation comes not from him but from one of them and if the separation becomes a fact before he is truly ready for it instead of remaining wishful thinking. Indeed, the adolescent may lose courage and hope when his parents separate and may believe that his own future is blighted.

Grief, Anger, and Guilt

A child will feel grief and anger if he is separated from his mother or father. While it is an oversimplification to liken the loss of a parent through divorce to loss through death, there is one aspect of separation through divorce that is particularly difficult. When a beloved person dies, the loss is acknowledged by everyone, and there is likely to be open mourning in the family. Mourning, painful though it is, marks the beginning of a healing process as well as the recognition that what is lost cannot be regained. But divorcing parents may not recognize and acknowledge the finality—or even the actuality—of their child's loss. The mother or father who remains at home with the child may exhibit relief or the joy of liberation. Even if he regrets the departure of the spouse, the adult may mourn in private so that the child is shut out. In that case the child may be denied the outlet of open grieving which could help to heal his sorrow.

Anger is often an intrinsic though unacknowledged factor in grief over the death of a beloved person. The survivor feels deserted by as well as bereft of the deceased. When parents separate, anger may well be prominent in their child's feelings. He may feel

bitterness at his departed parent's "desertion" and a fearful resentment toward the remaining parent for seeming to allow or even
to force the other to leave. Thus a child's love and loyalty to both
parents may be put under great strain. And as if sadness, grief, and
anger were not difficult enough to cope with, the child may well
believe that the separation is his fault.

In the fairy tales that have such powerful appeal for children,
while fortune and fate play a part in the unfolding of the story,
usually in the end the good are rewarded and the bad are pun-
ished. Such stories mirror the inner lives of children, especially
very young ones. At one and the same time they may feel totally
helpless and all-powerful. Their helplessness is evident—they
cannot feed, house, or clothe themselves without their parents'
providing the wherewithal. For the young child intense angry
feelings or persistent longings have a reality of their own. Their
power seems uncontrollable and is frightening because the child's
anger, wishes, or behavior seem to have led to the departure of a
parent. Thus, if a little girl has often exasperated her parents by
incessant demands at bedtime, she may believe that what is happening is well-deserved punishment for her behavior. She may
express this belief by saying that she will always go to bed without
making a fuss if only Mommy will come back home.

At a more profound level, all children, in the normal course
of growing up, at times harbor hostile wishes against their parents;
thus the little girl might at one time have felt, and might even have
said, that she wished Mommy would go away so that she could
have Daddy all to herself. When such "wishes" seem to come true,
children may naturally feel responsible because they have not yet
learned the crucial difference between wishing for something and
actively bringing it about. They may feel like the protagonist in
"Three Wishes," a story in which a good fairy grants the fulfill-
ment of three wishes to a discontented mortal who is at first

delighted, only to find after his first two wishes have been granted that he must use his last wish to undo what he had mistakenly thought he wanted so badly. But life is not a fairy tale, and a child's wish to undo the separation from his mother or father is not likely to be granted.

The Complexity of a Child's Response

Instead of allowing himself to experience his painful feelings directly as depression and helplessness, a child may show his reactions indirectly, by behavior changes. For example, the immediate result of a baby's all-pervasive sense of loss and deprivation may be disturbance of sleep, eating, and physical development. The most visible effect of the schoolchild's worry about who will look after him might be a sudden preoccupation with his health or a decline in school grades. The teenager's insecurity caused by not having the family he took for granted available as a safety net for his adolescent somersaults may lead to antisocial or delinquent behavior, an overly hectic social life, or premature sexual activity. These ways of acting out symbolize in dramatic form the adolescent's reaction to feeling cheated, left out, and powerless. Such behavior can also be a cry for affection and for reassurance about his masculinity to a boy and about her femininity to a girl.

The same behavior disturbances have different meanings at different ages in terms of the intensity of a child's reaction and what they portend for his development. A five-year-old child's return to bed-wetting is not as alarming as a twelve-year-old's. And a three-year-old's taking a candy bar from a drugstore counter is less worrisome than a teenager's shoplifting. Furthermore, some "bad" behavior is not necessarily an unhealthy manifestation any more than all "good" behavior is necessarily a positive sign, because what a child does or says does not always provide a straightforward clue to how he is affected by events, whether such events occur in an intact family or in a divorce situation.

For example, parents may find that when they return from a holiday, having left their child in the care of his grandmother, he is disobedient, rude, or excessively demanding—causing them to say with exasperation that it was almost not worthwhile to go away at all. They may be particularly annoyed because the grandmother reports that the child was good as gold and no trouble at all while they were away. But they probably should not conclude from this that their absence was a happier event for the child than their return. They might instead understand his behavior as a kind of revenge for their absence—a revenge that he can safely take only now that they have returned. A child sick in the hospital may be more fretful and weepy when his parents visit him than in their absence. This does not mean that he does not desperately want and need them to be with him—though the nurses may find him easier to manage when there are no visits. Parents are probably well aware how miserable the child was in their absence and are not misled by his behavior. In a moment of anger, a small child may threaten to run away from home and may even stomp out of the house. His mother and father are probably not unduly worried when this happens; they know that he will return in a short time because he truly knows that he needs them and that they care for him. They may perhaps be amused by the puzzled and slightly disappointed look on his face if, with mock seriousness, they offer to pack his clothes and make him a sandwich to speed him on his way. Similarly, if a little boy says to his mother after his father has left the family, "Don't worry, Mommy, I'll look after you now," this does not mean that he really thinks he is able to do so. And if a child behaves exceptionally well after his parents divorce and obeys their wishes without question, this does not necessarily indicate that the divorce has been a happy event for him. His amiability may be a manifestation of fear that he will be left or sent away, or of a hope that his goodness will be rewarded by the return of his absent parent.

Is the Separation of Unhappy Parents Good for a Child?

It is sometimes said that if a child has been surrounded by conflict, his parents' divorce is in his interest because an environment of strife or incompatibility interferes with his sense of trust and gives him a distorted model of how people can get along in a long-term relationship. The child, by this logic, is better off living in a tranquil single-parent home than in an emotionally divided two-parent household. But this is an oversimplification. One of the biggest threats to a child's security is the breakup of his family. While quarreling parents may distress him, this is in part because he anticipates and fears a family breakup, and it does not follow that the realization of his fear is easier for him than its continuance. Indeed, in some instances a child may have become so accustomed to the arguments, conflicts, and tensions created by warring parents that when they finally separate, he not only feels bereft of one parent but may actually miss the daily buildup of tension and its discharge in bouts of marital quarrels. For such a child the advantages of no longer living in a family in which there is unhappiness and strife are not immediately apparent. But the breakup of the family may be immediately experienced as catastrophic or massively threatening because it disrupts what he has learned to trust and interrupts the continuity of the only life he has known.

What you can do to help your child through this or any other difficult time will depend on your individual circumstances and attitude. Your child would not benefit if you were to behave in a manner which you do not find natural—"going by the book" (including this one) rather than following your own intuition about his and your needs and your accustomed way of interacting. Nor should you probe into his feelings or make psychological interpretations of his behavior. But your alertness to what your separation and divorce look like through the eyes of your child may point you in the direction of minimizing the complications that result from his efforts to come to terms with a situation over which he has no control and which constitutes a major upheaval in his life.

4

Telling Your Child

It Is Best to Be Honest

You should not mislead your child. Lies will confuse him and undermine his trust in you. This does not mean that you must—or even should—deliberately set out to air the details of your marital difficulties. But it does mean that you ought not to pretend, in response to his questions, that all is well when it is not. If he asks what is wrong, he deserves a truthful answer—that the two of you are not getting along well with each other. This is so even though your child, particularly if he is older, may worry about the possibility of your separating long before you decide to do so—perhaps because newspapers, television, and the experience of some of his friends have taught him that parents can and do split up. He should not be left to imagine and worry about what is wrong at home without having a chance to discuss his concerns openly with you. It is very troublesome to a child to observe tensions and disagreements but feel he is not supposed to know or talk about what is obvious to him. A child who cannot trust what he sees or hears may provide himself with even more fearful and upsetting explanations than the distressing reality. If, for instance, he has

25

already experienced the illness and death of a grandparent, he might imagine that one of you, or even he himself, is suffering from an incurable disease, and that is why everyone walks around with a long face. His fear might be fueled by a perfectly innocuous doctor's appointment, by his mother's pleading headaches to explain shutting herself into the bedroom, or by seeing his father take tablets for indigestion. Nameless dread is harder for a child to tolerate than facts, no matter how unpleasant the facts may be.

Once you have decided to separate permanently and one of you has left or is about to leave, your child ought to be told about it. He may find it difficult enough to accept and thereby come to terms with the finality of your separation without being told untruthfully that Daddy is going away on a long business trip or that Mommy is visiting Grandmother for a while because Grandmother is lonely. Even if he is very young you would be wise to tell him when one of you is about to leave and will not return home to live. Though the words spoken may mean little or nothing at the time, your tone of voice and accompanying hug and kiss can convey the message that something important is happening and at the same time give reassurance that one of you is there to stay. A small child tends to feel cheated and insecure even when his parents go out for an evening without saying goodbye. Such feelings are all the more likely if a mother or father leaves permanently, behind the child's back, as it were. He may still persist in believing that his absent parent will return, but, while you ought not to make a point of hammering the truth home repeatedly when he does not want to talk about it, you should not nourish his illusion by lying to him.

Not misleading your child does not mean that you should bombard him with a wealth of detail that he hasn't asked for and that may open up areas of worry he had not thought of. The truth about what is going on at home should be conveyed in a manner and at a time that are useful rather than overwhelming for your child. You can withhold details that you think he is unable to absorb or unwilling to know about. The line between what to say and what not to say cannot be defined in general terms. Rather, you should listen to and observe your child for clues to how much he wants to hear. But you should realize that it is not always possible to shield him from pain. For instance, your eight-year-old might ask you, "Why don't you and Daddy want to live together?" A straightforward answer—"Because we don't love each other any more"—may be more painful for him and more frightening than the separation itself. Why should he believe that his mother and father will continue to love him if they have not been able to love each other forever? You might, instead, reply, "Because we are unhappy living together," and perhaps he won't question any further. But if he persists with "Why are you un-happy?" you should reply truthfully. It is not your words but the facts that cause him pain. Avoiding his question or lying to him won't help. What you *can* do is to be sensitive to his pain and continue to show him the love you feel.

A United Front?

It is a good idea for both parents together to talk to your child if you can manage it. His bewilderment may be mitigated if he sees that the two of you can at least be united in the way you talk to him about his future. But if you find it too difficult to do this because, for instance, being in the same room with each other invariably leads to quarrels and recriminations which you do not want him to witness, it is helpful if you can at least discuss beforehand what you will say. For instance, if you, the mother, plan to tell your teenage daughter that her father is leaving the family because he has fallen in love with a younger woman, you, the father, may also want to tell her about this from your point of view. Or you may decide that both of you will tell your daughter only that you are unhappy living together without going into details, but that if she asks specific questions about whether one of you has fallen in love with someone else, you will not hide her father's involvement with the other woman.

You may well feel bitter and angry toward each other, and you may each be convinced that the other is entirely to blame for the failure of your marriage. Or one of you may feel predominantly angry and the other predominantly to blame. And perhaps your child, without being told to do so but simply on the basis of his own not necessarily accurate observations, takes sides between you. It is seldom easy for a child to do this without deep anguish, because he usually loves both his parents. Therefore, it may help him if you try not to show too much bitterness toward each other when you talk to him about your divorce. Of course, this may be extraordinarily difficult if not impossible while you are in the midst of intense turmoil yourselves. Perhaps one or both of you will share your anger with your child—either deliberately or because you simply cannot help it. You have your own needs and feelings as individuals and not just as parents, and your child can live with this reality. Nevertheless, if you are able to achieve enough distance from your own hurts so that each of you can think and speak of the other as your child's parent rather than merely as a disappointing spouse, you may make the situation more comfortable for him, especially if he can feel he can continue to love you both without offending or hurting either one of you.

What to Say

Children of all ages need to be reassured about their future. However, the details of what you say to your child will depend on his age and on the things that you know to be important to him.

Your three-year-old boy may need to hear that Daddy will read his favorite bedtime story each evening now that Mommy is going away, and his fourteen-year-old sister may want to know that someone will still drive her to weekly skating lessons.

When you talk about your separation, try to do it with words and ideas that your child can understand. You might think about what would have made sense to you when you were his age and what would have been most reassuring for you to hear under such circumstances. For example, a mother might say to her six-year-old son, "Daddy is not going to live here anymore, and you and I will stay by ourselves, but Daddy will come to see you often." A father might say to his ten-year-old daughter, "Your mother and I have not been getting along; we think we will all be happier if we don't live together anymore. We both love you just as much as ever, but you will go on living with your mother, and you and I will spend some time together every week." Or a father might tell his sixteen-year-old daughter, "I'm sure you know by now that things haven't been right between your mother and me for a long time. We have decided not to live together anymore and will probably get a divorce. Both of us want to look after you, of course, and perhaps you can stay with your mother some of the time and with me some of the time. In any event, we will try to work out the best possible arrangement with you, since whatever plan we make must also make sense from your point of view."

Of course, these examples are stilted and idealized over-simplifications. If a husband has left the house after beating his wife in a drunken rage, it is more important for her to assure her child that the two of them are safe than to go into lengthy explanations about his father's absence. Or if a mother has gone off to live with another man and his children, it will be most important for the father to reassure their child that he will continue to love and look after him and will not abandon him as well. Each set of parents and children have their own way of talking to each other, and you will find your own way of telling your child about your separation. You know him—his level of comprehension, his fears, fancies, and wishes. Though you should not give conflicting explanations to your children if you have more than one child, you should choose what you say to each on the basis of your knowledge of him. This need not mean that you can't talk to all your children at the same time. Each one will in any event hear and understand what you say in terms of his own capacity. The same information and even the same words will have different meanings for each child and consequently may stimulate different questions, which will give you a clue to what is important to each. You should trust your intuition and talk to each child in a way that you think makes sense for him and that at the same time is, if not comfortable, natural for you.

Your child may persist in questioning you far beyond what you consider reasonable. While you may not wish to answer his questions about a particular matter that you consider private, you should realize that he would not ask if he did not consider your response important. You may be able to get him to tell you what specific concerns prompted his question and address those directly. In any event, you should not evade his questions or stop talking about matters that concern him—such as where he will live, how often he will see the parent who is leaving, whether either of you plans to remarry, and what will happen to the dog.

Your Child Is Not to Blame

If your child asks you, "Is it my fault that Daddy left?" or says to you, "I'll always do what you tell me from now on if only you'll come back home," this may be your cue to assure him that he is not the cause of your separation.[1] His feeling of responsibility may persist in spite of your explanations, but it might be relieved and certainly should not be reinforced by what you have to say on the subject. For instance, if your quarrels have frequently centered on your child—arguments over discipline, for example—he may think that you would not have separated were it not for him. He needs to be told that it was not his behavior but your inability to get along with each other that brought about your separation. Of course, you yourselves might believe that your marriage would in fact have survived had you remained childless, perhaps because there would have been fewer quarrels about money if you had been free of child-related expenses or because there would have been no occasion to quarrel about how to bring up your child. Or perhaps there were special problems with your child, such as a serious illness, learning difficulties, or involvement with drugs, that subjected your marriage to greater strains than it could withstand. If that is the case, verbal assurances that he is not to blame are not likely to be persuasive.

If your child does not say anything about being responsible for your divorce you probably should not raise the subject with him even if you suspect that he harbors such feelings, perhaps because you know that he has often heard you quarrel about him. You might want to tell him that you are getting divorced because you are unhappy with each other. At some time you might make a general comment to the effect that the reasons people divorce usually have nothing to do with their children. And you can tell him from time to time how proud and happy you both are to have him for a child. But you ought not to pry into his emotions or insist that he discuss them with you. Your child is entitled to privacy no less than you are. More than that, even if your surmise about his hidden feelings is correct, you may be doing him a disservice by forcing them out into the open. It would be likely to hinder rather than help his resolution of internal conflicts, whether these are accentuated by your divorce or not, if you were to expose thoughts and feelings that he is not ready to confront or wants to keep to himself.

Once May Not Be Enough

You may have braced yourself for a long time before talking to your child about your impending separation and divorce. You may have found breaking the news extremely distressing and feel enormously relieved when you have finally done it. Nevertheless, you should be prepared to discuss these events many more times even if the child initially accepts your announcement and whatever explanation you give him without question. What your divorce means to your child is not static but changes as he grows older and in terms of his actual life experience. Your preschooler may not be sufficiently articulate to discuss his concerns; your older child may be too hurt, embarrassed, afraid, or resentful to talk about them with you. You may wish to provide him with opportunities to do so, though you should not force him to confide in you or to talk about matters that he does not wish to discuss. If he is able and willing to talk with you about his fears, anger, uncertainty, and preferences, this may help him to come to terms with the inevitable turmoil of your divorce. The important thing is for you to be available to talk further if and when he is ready to do so.

Above all, your child needs to be assured that you love him in spite of your separation and will continue to do so; for even if he does not think that the separation was his fault, he may feel that you cannot love him as much as he thought you did or you would not be separating. Of course, if your spouse has abandoned you and your child without a word, it may be neither honest nor helpful to try to convince him of his absent parent's abiding love.

But when it is realistic, your child needs to hear many times and, more importantly, needs to feel that his parents love him. And you should not be too surprised if, long after you think you have made it abundantly clear that there will be no reconciliation, long after one or both of you have remarried, for that matter, your child still hopes that the two of you will get together again. This may be his fondest wish, and such wishes die hard.

PART II.
Getting Your Divorce

5

With Whom Should Your Child Live? Agreeing on Custody

Your divorce puts the legal stamp of finality on the restructuring of your old family relationships. But from your child's point of view it is often only the formal recognition of changes which have long been under way. You, his parents, may have made and implemented custody choices from the moment that you stopped living together, and perhaps even before then. If the two of you can agree on custody—whether you opt for single-parent or joint custody—you will minimize the role of the court and maximize your child's ability to sustain a sound relationship with both of you.

The divorce decree will be in the form of an order specifying which of you is to be primarily responsible for the care and upbringing of your child by "awarding" or "granting" custody to one of you, or it may grant custody to both of you jointly. It will also specify the rights of the "noncustodial" parent with respect to the amount of time he or she can spend with the child ("visitation rights") and the extent to which he or she can participate in making choices about schooling, medical care, religious upbringing, and other matters. Thus, the decree determines not only who

37

is to have custody but also the conditions of custody. By so doing it can affect the day-to-day lives of the whole family. Most judges realize that they cannot learn as much about the two of you and your child at a court hearing as you yourselves know. Therefore, they will generally accept a written or oral separation agreement presented by the parents and make it the basis of their custody order.

Choosing Single-Parent Custody

Perhaps in your case the custody choice is an easy one to make. One of you may be unwilling or unable to look after your child. You, the father, may have left your family for another woman who refuses to have your child live with her. Or, you, the mother, may have decided that you must go into the world to find yourself and do not wish to be burdened with responsibility for your small child. Or one of you may be suffering from a disabling disease. The choice may also be easy because, even though both of you would have liked custody, you agree that your child would be better off with one of you than the other. Thus, you, the father, may know that the demands of your job will frequently take you away from home for long periods of time so that you would have to rely on someone else for his day-to-day care, and you may reluctantly conclude that he would be better off living with his mother. Or you, the mother, may realize that you are having a great deal of difficulty setting necessary limits for your teenager and may agree to let your husband have custody because he is better at this. Or the two of you may have decided to be guided by what you know to be your child's preference.

But perhaps your choice is not simple. You may both want what is best for your child and be willing and able to assume custody, and you believe you can cooperate in making and carrying out a wise custody choice. But you may be unsure of what in fact would be the best arrangement for your child. If that is your situation you might want to think about how you would answer the following questions:

Do both of you want the responsibility for your child, or is one of you asking for custody because that is the expected thing to do, because you are afraid that your child will reproach you for leaving him with the other parent, because you feel guilty, or because your friends or your own parents—your child's grandparents— are pressing you to ask for custody?

Which parent has provided most of the day-to-day care? Which parent has fed and diapered the baby? Which parent has prepared meals for the toddler and taken him to the park? Which parent has put him to bed at night and got him dressed in the morning? Which parent helps the schoolchild with homework? Which parent comforts the child when he is unhappy? The younger your child, the more important it is that there be continuity of care by the same parent. If both of you have regularly shared in looking after your child— whatever his age—the answers to this set of questions will not solve your dilemma, though they may point in the direction of both of you continuing to share responsibility if you think you can cooperate to make this work.

Which parent would find it easier to be a single parent without the daily physical and emotional support of the other parent?

Which parent is more likely to remain in the neighborhood where the child's school and friends are?

If it is not a financial necessity for both of you to work, *which parent is more likely to be able to earn enough money that the other can stay at home with the young child should he or she desire to do so?*

Which parent can manage to care for all the children, if you have more than one? In most cases it is better for children not to be separated from each other when their parents divorce. Your children, even if they constantly argue and fight with each other, are likely to be united in times of trouble and can give each other comfort and help in their new situation.

Which parent is more willing and more likely to be consistent in the desire to look after the child until adulthood?

Which parent is more likely to encourage and provide the opportunity for regular visits with the other parent and to accept such contact without making the child feel disloyal?

If you consider these questions from your child's perspective and can agree on your answers—if you see your relationships to your child in the same way—they may point you in the right direction. Though it is not easy to know all the factors to consider or how much weight to give to each, such questions can focus your thinking on what your child needs and may help you to make a wise choice for him.

If you want to do what is best for your child, it is a great deal easier for you to recognize what should *not* determine your choice. For example, it is not helpful to your child, and may be damaging to him, for one or both of you to use the custody choice to punish the other for a miserable marriage or for ending what was a happy one. You, the father, may feel, for instance, that because your wife left you for another man, she should not be allowed to have your child as well. That is an understandable reaction, but it may obscure consideration of what is important for your child—whether his mother has been more involved than you in his day-to-day care, whether she has been a good mother to him, how much he would miss her daily presence, and whether she and her new partner want to have him live with them. Again, though financial considerations may be important to you, as far as possible they should not determine the custody choice. Thus, if you, the father, believe it will cost you less to take care of your child yourself than to pay child support to your wife, this is not a good primary reason, from your child's point of view, for you to have custody. Similarly, if you, the mother, believe that your husband is more likely to keep up mortgage payments on your house if your child lives with you, that ought not to be your main reason for seeking custody.

Choosing Joint Custody

Joint custody is an arrangement characteristic of marriage. Mother and father live together, more or less in harmony. Both are entitled to make choices for their child and participate in caring for him. How much sharing there is in practice is a matter of individual preference or necessity. Some mothers and fathers present a united front to their child while others do not, but differences are routinely settled (or left unresolved) without resort to law. Divorce ends this automatic joint custody, probably in practice and certainly in the legal sense. The marriage has broken up and "custody" has to be allocated formally.

Post-divorce joint custody is viewed by many as a viable and perhaps preferable alternative to the traditional arrangement of granting custody to either mother or father and visitation rights to the noncustodial parent.[1] Advocates of joint custody argue that it is good for the child because it means less interruption in the continuity of care by both parents; because it avoids the "weekend parent" syndrome in which the visiting parent and his child find it difficult to sustain a meaningful relationship; and because it makes it harder for a vindictive custodial parent to put obstacles in the way of the child's maintaining contact with his other parent. All this can be true for you if the joint custody arrangement is one that both of you like and continue to like. But it may work against rather than for your child's interest if one of you opposes it and it is implemented only by court order and under the threat of contempt proceedings.

You may want to consider joint custody as the arrangement of your choice. After all, you might reason, you are divorcing each other, not your child. He loves and needs both of you equally, and both of you want to look after him and are equally qualified by temperament and experience to do so. If that is your view, there is an infinite variety of possible arrangements for you to think about, for the phrase "joint custody" (a term sometimes used interchangeably with "shared custody," "divided custody," or "alternating custody") covers not one particular and easily identifiable living situation but, rather, a broad spectrum of parents' participation in raising their child.

Some post-divorce joint custody arrangements are virtually indistinguishable from traditional post-divorce one-parent custody. For instance, you might agree that your child is to live with his mother and that his father will see him several times a week, look after him on weekends and holidays, and participate in making decisions on such matters as religious education and whether he should have braces on his teeth. Though this is not a full sharing of child-rearing, you might feel that this type of joint custody has psychological advantages that make it preferable to single-parent custody, no matter how little practical difference there may be between them. If the father is not denigrated to an inferior legal status, it may be easier for him to accept the fact that the child lives with his mother most of the time; and he may, in turn, be more likely to visit regularly and often and to keep up with support payments. And the child may be less likely to feel that his father has voluntarily given him up—abandoned him.

Other joint custody arrangements differ substantially from traditional single-parent custody. You might agree, for instance, that your child is to live with his mother Monday through Wednesday of each week and with his father Thursday through Sunday; or that he will spend six months of each year with his mother and six months with his father. This would mean, of course, not only that the two of you must consult each other about extraordinary decisions but that you would each at times be solely responsible for such day-to-day tasks as feeding and dressing your baby, toilet-training your toddler, sending your older child off to school, and listening to your adolescent's complaints.

If you are thinking about some form of joint custody, you might want to ask yourselves some questions that touch on your capacity to tolerate the arrangement and your child's ability to benefit from it:

> Can the two of you put aside your animosity and bitterness toward each other sufficiently to join in making decisions for your child? If you cannot, he will suffer under the intolerable stress of trying to be loyal to two adults who are in conflict with each other.
>
> Did your quarrels as husband and wife frequently

center on matters connected with your child's upbringing, or was that not one of the areas of dispute? If you could not agree about such matters before your separation, do you nevertheless believe that you will be able to agree afterwards because the daily irritations of living with each other will have been eliminated?

Are you fairly certain that once you are separated and your child is the only contact between the two of you the same inability to get along with each other (even if not centered on the child) that led to your separation will not persist or reappear in your efforts to cooperate in planning and caring for him? Do you believe that once you are free from the strain of living with each other disputes will be less likely? Do both of you have the same, or at least not conflicting, moral and ethical standards to convey to your child? Do you have similar attitudes toward school, homework, money, health care, watching television, bedtimes, and sex?

If your child is to divide his time between the two of you, will the move be made every day, every week, every school term, or every year? Will your child move from one house to the other, or will he stay in the same house or apartment while the two of you rotate in and out (an arrangement sometimes referred to as "bird nesting")?

If the two of you are to do the moving, are you prepared to put up with the inconvenience without resentment toward your child for causing it?

If your child is to do the moving, is he likely to tolerate this well? Your infant might move easily from place to place, provided that his caregiving parent goes along with him. But he may find it more difficult when there is a change in the person who looks after him as well as a change of location. Your older child might find it easier to be cared for by the two of you alternately but may be more attached to his own room, furniture, and neighborhood.[2] If your child is of school age, are you both prepared to live in the same school district? If not, what school will he attend? Or do you expect him to attend two different schools alternately?[3] Will he need two sets of school books and clothes? Or will he carry these and his favorite toys and other belongings from place to place?

What will your attitude toward joint custody be if one of you remarries or moves in with another person of the opposite sex? Or of the same sex if he or she is a homosexual?

If the joint custody arrangement you have agreed on should not work out well, whether because one of you must move, because your child reacts badly, or because one or both of you simply cannot tolerate the arrangement for some reason, are you prepared to settle peaceably on another arrangement in your child's interest? Or is your attitude "either this or we go to court!"? If the latter, have you thought about and discussed with your lawyer what a judge might be likely to decide?[4] And what a court battle and a court-imposed custody arrangement might mean to your child?

If you can work out the answers to such questions together; or if you decide that, no matter what difficulties may arise in the future, you will solve them when the time comes because you both believe that it is of overriding importance for your child not to lose a parent through your separation; or even if you choose joint custody because either or both of you fear that you would lose custody to the other in a court battle and believe that joint custody is better than no custody at all—then joint custody may work well for your child and minimize the disruption in his life. Otherwise, joint custody may add to his difficulties. He will be likely to suffer from family dissension just as he did before your separation. Instead of having two parents to whom he can look for security and authority, he may in effect not even have one whole parent, since neither of you will be fully in charge, and you may be pulling in different directions. If your conflict continues after your separation you may be quite unable to avoid using him as a weapon in your continued war. And in his frustrated search for security, your child, especially as he gets older, may learn to play one of you off against the other in order to reassure himself for a moment that he can control his life by getting what he wants, at least in terms of material things or rules of behavior. While such undesirable consequences for a child are certainly possible in single-parent custody as well, the opportunity and temptation to bring them about are likely to be greater with joint custody.

Counseling or Mediation to Help You Reach Agreement

If you and your spouse are having trouble agreeing about custody, you might try formal or informal counseling or mediation rather than immediately each retaining a lawyer to negotiate an agreement. You might find it useful to see your minister or rabbi, or a relative or friend in whose good sense you trust, to discuss the separation and custody. Or you might prefer to consult a professional counselor. Counseling may help you to clarify your feelings and to focus on your child's welfare rather than on your animosity toward your spouse, so that the two of you can reach a sensible agreement. But though you may find counseling helpful, in the final analysis you should feel free to reject the advice you receive if you do not agree with it, whether it is professional or informal. Accepting advice about custody matters is different from, for example, deferring to the judgment of a doctor or mental health therapist to whom you have taken your child for diagnosis and treatment. Professional expertise is not necessary to raise a child. You probably know your child, yourself, and your spouse better than even the ablest and best-qualified professional or the best-motivated and most understanding of friends. Above all, it is you and your child, not the advice giver, who must live with the choices you make. Only if they make sense to you are they likely to work out well for your child.

Mediation focuses even more directly than counseling on arriving at a specific custody agreement. A professional mediator meets with divorcing spouses, either together or in separate sessions, to help them sort out their differences about custody and financial matters and reach a compromise. Mediation usually costs less than retaining two separate lawyers, but the trade-off is that you forego the single-minded advocacy that you have the right to expect from your own lawyer.[5] There are private mediators in most communities and on the staffs of some law offices. Also, a number of courts now offer mediation services.[6]

Before you decide to participate in a conference with a court-employed mediator, you would be wise to find out whether he is limited to helping you resolve your differences or is also authorized or required to make a custody recommendation to the judge if his mediation efforts fail. From a child's point of view, mediation is useful only if it is voluntary and results in a custody arrangement that both parents have come to accept as reasonable. If mediation is a condition of access to the court or if the mediator's recommendations can be imposed over the objections of a parent, the child is likely to be no better off than when a judge makes the custody decision after a heated court battle.

6

Using Your Lawyer to Advantage

Even if the two of you have worked out custody and financial matters without help from a lawyer, each of you will most likely find yourself consulting one in the course of your divorce to help you cope with the mechanics of the court system and probably also to prepare your separation agreement in suitable form for presenting to the judge. If you have been unable to reach agreement it is all the more important that you have legal counsel. An understanding of the scope as well as the limits of your lawyer's role will enable you to use to advantage the help he can give you in looking out for your child's interests as well as your own.

A Separate Lawyer for Each Spouse

When parents separate, the same family income must often be stretched to support two households instead of one, unless and until a nonworking spouse enters the job market. You undoubtedly regard legal fees as an unwelcome additional burden. You may question the need for two lawyers for one divorce.

Suppose a couple has agreed that they want to end their marriage, that the mother will have custody of the child and remain in the family home, that the father can see the child as often as he likes and will pay X dollars annually for the support of mother and child. Why can't this couple go to one lawyer together and simply ask him to write all this in the legal language of a separation agreement, ready to be submitted to a judge as the basis of the divorce decree? The answer is that this is probably not a good time for either of them to do without legal advice, and a lawyer may not and cannot properly advise two clients who may have conflicting interests.

In spite of the understanding that divorcing spouses may have reached, their interests may be or may become to some extent conflicting. The time of separation may be so emotionally charged that one of them agrees to something under pressure from the other in face-to-face discussion which he or she would not have agreed to under calmer or perhaps less intimidating circumstances. For instance, a mother might agree to joint custody because her husband has convinced her that if she does not he will stop giving her money to live on. Or a father might agree to excessively large payments because his wife threatens that if he does not she will never let him see his child.

Also, one or both of the spouses may not be fully aware of their rights or obligations under the laws of their state, or of the implications of what they have agreed to. Thus, a husband might not realize that fathers are not automatically excluded from consideration for custody, nor mothers from having to make child support or alimony payments. He might not realize that the payments he has agreed to make can be considered either "alimony" or "child support" or some of each, depending on the exact terms of the agreement; that "alimony" if structured in a certain way may be income to the wife for federal income tax purposes and deductible by the husband on his federal income tax return, whereas "child support" may be neither income to her nor deductible by him. He might not realize that he could arrange alimony payments to continue until the death of the wife or to end with her remarriage or, perhaps, if she "cohabits" with another man without marrying him; to terminate upon his own death or remain as an obligation on his estate; to go up or down depending on husband's and wife's earnings; to go up annually at a fixed percentage or to go up proportionately with increases in the cost of living; or to combine or ignore these and other factors. Similarly, child support payments could, by agreement, terminate when the child reaches majority or continue until his college education is paid for.

A wife may not be aware of the type of alimony and property awards she could expect from a judge if no agreement was reached.

A husband may not realize that if he deeds the family home to his wife he may remain liable on the mortgage debt and that this may make it difficult or impossible for him to obtain a mortgage should he wish to buy another house. He may not have thought through what is to happen if his wife decides after a while that she does not want to stay in the house. How are the proceeds of the sale to be divided? If, on the other hand, she should wish to stay in the house even after the child has grown up, should she be allowed to do so without compensating the husband, especially if the house was the couple's main or only asset at the time of the divorce? Or should she be required to sell the house so that the proceeds can be distributed in whatever proportion they agree on?

This is by no means an exhaustive list of areas of possible conflict, nor is it an analysis of federal tax laws pertaining to divorce (which, in any event, are always subject to change). It is a lawyer's task to advise his client of the possible implications and ramifications of negotiated divorce agreements. How such issues should be resolved, what should be included in an agreement, and the advantages of different provisions to the mother, the father, and the child vary from state to state and, more important, from family to family. You might think that issues such as these are minor details in the context of your overall agreement—typical legal nitpicking. But what seems unimportant to you now may assume importance with the passage of time. If the two of you use only one lawyer, and he fails to point out something you had not thought about at the time of your separation or the agreement later turns out to be more advantageous to one of you, the other is likely to believe that the lawyer, rather than having been a neutral scribe, in fact drew a one-sided agreement.

Even if you think that you can work out custody and visitation arrangements without legal help, because you believe that these matters are less technical than financial issues, you should bear in mind that if the financial portion of your agreement is unsatisfactory to one of you, it may very well lead to disputes over custody and visitation which you would rather spare your child. It is therefore in your child's interest as well as your own that both parents are satisfied with the financial settlement.

Of course, the fact that there are potential problems inherent in agreements reached by separating couples does not mean that you should not try to settle property and support as well as custody matters between yourselves. On the contrary, and especially from your child's point of view, this is likely to lead to a much more sensible and effective settlement than one imposed by a judge—a stranger who has little knowledge of the needs and capacities of your family. But your agreement may more truly reflect the wishes and realistic prospects of both of you—or at any rate be something that you and your child can live with—if each of you goes over its provisions and their possible legal consequences with your own lawyer. However, you should remain in charge. Do not allow the lawyer to create an atmosphere of strife where none existed. Do not let him discourage you from reaching amicable agreement. Get him to help you to do so by giving you a realistic picture of what a judge is likely to order if he must make the decision for you. If you tell your lawyer that the two of you have agreed in principle on what you consider fair and neither of you is looking for a legal victory in court, he should limit himself to asking questions, clarifying details, pointing out legal and practical consequences, and seeing to it that the agreement is put into writing as clearly as possible so as to avoid future misunderstandings. If, on the other hand, it transpires that, for example, you, the wife, actually feel cheated or browbeaten by your husband, then it may be well for your lawyer to attempt to negotiate the differences with your husband's lawyer rather than have you go to court with an agreement which is one in name only and is likely to lead to future disputes.

Selecting Your Lawyer

Select your lawyer with care. Perhaps a friend can recommend someone with whom he or she had a good experience. Or the local bar association can provide a list of lawyers who handle divorces. Once you have a name, make an appointment for a consultation, ask what this will cost, and find out whether the consultation charge will be applied toward the fee for the whole divorce if you decide to hire this lawyer. If you think you cannot afford to pay for a lawyer, you can consult your legal aid office to find out whether you are eligible for free legal services.

You should use your first appointment not only to ask questions but also to form an opinion of the lawyer. If he is going to represent you, you should feel at ease with him, though you don't necessarily have to be enamored of his personality. Some women may not feel comfortable discussing intimate marriage details with a male lawyer; others may feel that only a male lawyer can be tough enough to protect their interests. Some men may have similar preferences for or prejudices against male or female lawyers. Perhaps your lawyer's gender is a matter of indifference to you, but you find his manner unsympathetic. Or you may not believe that what he tells you about your legal prospects can really be so. Or he may quote a higher fee than you think fair or affordable. If you have strong negative feelings about the lawyer after your first telephone call or appointment, do not hesitate to try another one. Shop around for a lawyer until you find one in whom you have confidence, because if he is to do a good job for you, you must be open and truthful with him and be prepared to trust his judgment on legal matters. Changing lawyers in midstream may be unpleasant and costly and will undoubtedly delay the divorce proceedings. Nevertheless, if you are truly dissatisfied with the way your lawyer is handling your divorce, you are free at any time to replace him.

Consulting a Lawyer before Your Separation

If you are thinking about getting a divorce, or if your spouse has told you that he or she wants one, you may want advice on the legal implications and procedures of separation and divorce. For instance, if you are the mother of young children and have not worked outside the home, you may need to know how to arrange to get support payments from your husband pending the decree, how soon you can get them, and how much you are likely to get. You may need information about local, state, or federal benefits for which you might be eligible. You may also need advice on how to serve divorce papers on an irate spouse, whether and how the law of your state can give you and your children physical protection against an abusive husband, and whether you can get a court to order him to leave the house. If you fear for your own or your child's safety because your husband has in the past been physically abusive or has threatened to kill you or your child if you attempt to leave or file for divorce, your lawyer may be able to put you in touch with a "battered women's shelter" in your community.[1] If you are considering a divorce but cannot bear the thought of separating from your children, you may need to find out what your chances of getting custody are if your case goes to court as a contested matter. If your lawyer tells you your chances are good this may help you decide whether to go ahead with the divorce or whether to press for custody if you cannot reach agreement with your spouse. Or your lawyer may tell you that there is no way of predicting the outcome of a custody battle in your case. In any event, he can advise you on how to maximize your chances. For instance, if you, the mother, want custody and also want to leave your husband immediately, he will probably suggest that you take your children with you when you leave, even though this makes it more difficult for you to find an affordable place to live.

There are probably a great many things you will want to find out from your lawyer: an explanation of your state's divorce laws; whether, even though it is generally no longer necessary to prove that one spouse has been at "fault" in order to get a divorce—by, for example, "mental cruelty" or committing adultery—"fault" can be considered by a judge in your state in awarding custody, alimony, and support; how long it takes to get a divorce; and what takes place at a court hearing.

You may be quite nervous during your first consultation and may tend to forget some of what you wanted to ask. Therefore, it is a good idea to get your questions ready before you see the lawyer and come armed with a written list. If you do not understand something he says to you, make him explain it until you do. Do not put up with legal jargon; everything you need to know can be explained in simple language.

You should answer your lawyer's questions frankly unless he cannot explain to your satisfaction in what way they are relevant. Nothing you say is going to shock him; everything you tell him is confidential, and he cannot give you reliable answers to your own questions if you withhold important information.

Advice from a Lawyer about Nonlegal Matters

You, the unhappy husband or wife, may find it a great relief to pour out your feelings to your lawyer, who is your ally in this difficult period. You may be tempted to ask his advice about nonlegal divorce-related problems involving you and your child. And some—though by no means all—lawyers are sympathetic listeners. However, it is wise for you to remember that your lawyer is a stranger who probably does not know much about you and your family personally. He is more qualified to advise you on *how* to get a divorce than on *whether* to get one. And he is usually not trained as a family guidance counselor or psychiatrist. He may respond to you out of his own experience as a human being and parent, but this is not professional advice. If he thinks it appropriate, he might properly ask you whether you have considered getting psychiatric or other help and may refer you to community or private doctors or agencies if you are interested. Some lawyers, in fact, work in association with a mental health therapist or counselor. But your lawyer is generally not qualified to diagnose whether you need help. If you need professional advice on nonlegal matters, you should be cautious about accepting it from your lawyer.

Your Lawyer's Role in Representing Your Interests as Spouse and Parent in Negotiations and in Court

Once you have decided on separation and divorce you may still look to your lawyer for information and perhaps advice but now you also need him to be your advocate. He will negotiate with your spouse's lawyer, prepare your separation agreement, and present it to the judge, or, if you have been unable to reach an agreement about custody or financial matters, plead your case in court.

It is a good idea to ask your lawyer to explain the implications of the conduct of your case not only for you but also for your child. Without ever thinking about it, you, like most parents, probably assume that you represent your child's interests as well as your own. "What is good for me is good for my child." And this is usually true, because above all children need parents who are in charge and who insulate them from control by outsiders; thus, particular decisions affecting a child's life are left to his parents' discretion unless they violate child neglect or abuse laws or some other general law such as that requiring school attendance. For example, parents are not prevented by any law from moving with their children from one part of the country to another or to a different country,[2] whether in order to get a better job or to live near a gambling casino. Nor does any outsider have the right to interfere with a family's lifestyle that perhaps causes a child to be separated for long periods of time from one or both parents because he is sent away to school or to live with a grandmother, or is left in the care of a succession of paid housekeepers.

But in the divorce situation the picture may change because "parents" are now split into a mother and a father who may be in conflict, and one of whom may assume greater importance in the child's life than the other. One result is that your adversary interest as a divorcing spouse may not always be the same as your interest as a parent who wants what is best for your child. For example, anger at your spouse or the desire to avoid feeling guilty about leaving your family are, from your child's vantage point, not necessarily good reasons for your getting custody. Further, the best legal strategy for you to win custody may have negative implications for your child.

Assume, for instance, that you are the mother of a two-year-old boy of whom both you and your husband wish to have custody. Your husband has been having an affair with another woman and has moved out of the house and initiated the divorce proceedings. He has been a loving father and you do not object strenuously to his continuing to see your son after the divorce, although you would prefer that there be no contact. Your husband, through his lawyer, has made a motion in court for an interim visitation order—he seeks reasonable visitation, pending a resolution of the custody dispute. Assume further that before the separation you and your husband have shared the day-to-day care of the child. Your son is equally attached to and dependent on both of you and it would, in effect, be a toss-up as to which parent he would be better off with, although he would clearly be best off with both of you if you were united. If your lawyer thinks only of your legal interest in obtaining custody at the final hearing, he might advise you to oppose your husband's interim visitation and to drag out the final hearing so that it does not take place for at least a year. By that time, if there have been no visits, the father will probably have been transformed from a source of comfort and love into a virtual stranger. And because custody decisions generally take a child's need for continuity of care into account and recognize that his sense of time is different from that of an adult, this might be just the factor that swings the custody award to you. But if your lawyer—either on his own or at your request—

also considers the effect of the strategy on your child, he might explore with you the possible advantages to the child of continuing to see his father. If the court should ultimately award custody to the father, it would probably be difficult enough for your son to separate from you without in addition moving in with a person who is a virtual stranger to him. If, on the other hand, the custody award should go to you, even though by this time you might have no objections to visits from the father and might actually welcome them—and even though such visits would probably be ordered over your objections anyway—it might be difficult for the child to reestablish a parental bond with his father.

As another example, if you, the father, believe that your ten-year-old daughter could tell the judge some things about her mother that might influence the custody decision in your favor, you might consider and discuss with your lawyer the burden the little girl would bear if she were asked to take sides between her parents.

It is important that you know what your lawyer's role is in relation to you and your child. In representing you, the parent, his role is twofold. He is, or can be, your counselor—your adviser—as well as your advocate. In the above examples, he can and should explore with you, mother or father, the pros and cons of opposing and not opposing interim visits and of having a child testify or not, in terms not only of the likely effect on the outcome of your case but also of what it might mean from the child's point of view. If you then ask your lawyer, "What do *you* think I ought to do?" he, in his role as your adviser, may properly express his preferences for or against subordinating your child's interest to the best strategy for your winning custody. Even if you do not specifically ask his advice, he may still volunteer his opinion, if you do not object. But if you either do not want to hear his opinion or do not wish to follow his advice, your lawyer properly has only two options. He can either inform you that he no longer wishes to represent you, or, in his role as your advocate, he must represent your wishes to the best of his ability—and the interest of the child as seen by *you*, the mother or father. This is so even if he personally does not agree with you, whether because he believes you are jeopardizing your case in the interest of your child's well-being or because he thinks you are not sufficiently concerned with your child. You do not want a lawyer who represents you in a lackluster manner, who, for example, either deliberately or inadvertently sends signals to the judge that he thinks the father should have interim visitation rights even though you, the mother who is his client, oppose them; or that he thinks you do not deserve custody because of your selfish attitude.

Do not be intimidated by your lawyer; after all, you, not he, must bring up your child. Nor is he a child development expert to whom you have gone for advice. Do not hesitate to ask him forthrightly whether he will do his best for you even though he disagrees with you. If you get any inkling that he will not defer to your wishes, find another lawyer.

This is quite different from the lawyer's possible insistence, for instance, that interim visits not be opposed, or that the little girl not testify because, even without taking the impact on the child into account, it would do his adult client's case more harm than good. An assessment of whether a particular legal strategy would or would not enhance your chance of winning your case is part of his job as your advocate. If, however, your lawyer appears oblivious to the possible impact of his strategy on your child, it is up to you to evaluate this when deciding whether or not to follow his advice.

7

The Custody Hearing and the Judge's Custody Order

If the Two of You Have Agreed on Custody

Judges seldom reject or alter a custody agreement reached by the parents even though by law they may have the power to do so.[1] One judge may routinely disapprove joint custody "bird-nesting" agreements in which mother and father take turns moving in and out of the house or apartment where the child lives because he does not think such arrangements can be good for any child. Another may reject agreements giving custody to mother or father alone because he believes that joint custody is best for all children. But such intervention is relatively rare. In general judges recognize that parents are best suited to decide what is best for their children and will accept whatever custody agreement parents or their lawyers present to them in court, as long as they are satisfied that both mother and father understand what they have agreed to. But when parents have been unable to reach agreement—when custody is contested—judges must themselves select and order a custody arrangement. In addition to designating the custodial parent, they may also specify the rights and responsibilities of both parents in such matters as support obligations and visits with the child.

If You Cannot Agree—Rules of Law for Custody Decisions

Divorce laws in the United States tie custody awards to "the best interests of the child." But there is little agreement about what that phrase means, or how "best interests" can be ascertained and implemented. In some instances the law has attempted to flesh out "best interests." The so-called tender years presumption, for instance, required judges in most cases to award the custody of young children to their mothers, on the theory that mothers are better qualified than fathers to look after small children. This made the judge's task easier and the outcome fairly predictable since there was no need to hear a large body of testimony on who the better parent was. The "tender years" presumption has been eroding. Men are asserting, and the law is beginning to recognize, that fathers can be good "mothers" even for very young children. But the underlying premise of this maternal preference—that a child needs continuity of care—has reemerged where the law requires judges to favor the child's "primary caretaker" or "primary psychological parent." That criterion may not be so easy to implement and the outcome may not be so predictable as when a presumption was made in favor of the mother. Some state laws authorize or even require judges to reintroduce "fault" into "no fault" divorces by looking to "reasons for the divorce" as one of the criteria on which to base custody awards. This not only complicates the judge's task but would also seem to contravene the "best interests" standard, since there is no necessary correlation between being the "spouse not at fault" and being the better parent.

No matter which rules of law they must apply, conscientious judges often find the making of custody decisions a difficult assignment. Divorcing parents sometimes complain of a judge's insensitive and unsympathetic attitude. In fact what the judge probably feels is frustration, worry, and bewilderment because he has too large a case load, because he knows how important his decision is to a child's well-being, and because in many cases he cannot find the "right" answer in spite of, or perhaps because of, voluminous testimony and opinions by child experts.

Judges can, but often do not, cut through the complexity of their task by keeping in mind some general observations that apply to all children and do not require the opinions of child experts in each case. If in deciding which parent should have custody of a child the judge recognizes that neither he nor anyone else can accurately predict what will happen in the distant future, he will not sacrifice present benefits out of fear of future harm, or vice versa. If a six-year-old girl has been fed, dressed, and generally looked after by her father while her mother, for whatever reason, did not participate very much in her day-to-day care, the judge should not be deterred from awarding custody to the father by his belief that teenage girls need to look to their mothers for guidance and are better off not living in an all-male household. Even assuming this to be true, by the time the child reaches her teens the father may have remarried a woman with three daughters, the mother may have died, or any number of unpredictable events may have occurred. But what *can* accurately be predicted is that if the child is forcibly separated from her father she will suffer here and now, and the judge can protect her from this by awarding him custody. Or, if a three-year-old boy's well-being is threatened by his alcoholic mother's behavior, the judge should not deny custody to the father because of a medical prediction that the mother will be completely "cured" in two years' time. If the child is to thrive he cannot afford to wait for good care in the future—he needs it here and now. And if the judge also recognizes that in many custody disputes both husband and wife are fit parents and the child may be substantially attached to both of them, he will not attempt to do what he is not qualified to do by legal training or judicial experience—namely, to make fine distinctions between degrees of fitness and attachment so as to choose the "right" parent. In such cases lengthy investigations and deliberations are not likely to yield a more conclusive or trustworthy basis for decision-making. Indeed, they are likely to be detrimental to the child's well-being because they prolong the inevitable period of uncertainty about the future. Where there is little means to choose between parents, judges can best serve the interests of children by making a speedy decision, no matter which parent they select. But the fact that mother and father appear equally qualified because they have shared equally in their child's upbringing while living together should not lead to an automatic joint custody order requiring them to share in the child's upbringing after the divorce. Unless both parents are willing and able to cooperate in such an arrangement, it will only expose the child to continuing conflict and, from his point of view, provide the worst rather than the best resolution of the custody dispute.

When circumstances are such that the application of general principles does not yield an easily ascertainable answer, judges can look to a variety of sources for information on where a particular child's best interests lie.

Court-ordered Custody Investigations

If the judge in your case has the court personnel available he might order a custody investigation of the character, habits, and living arrangements of mother and father and of their relationship with the child. He might rely heavily on the resulting recommendations because the investigation was "impartial"—that is, conducted by an individual employed by the court rather than by one of the adversaries—and also because he thinks the facts found by the investigator are likely to be more reliable than the testimony of husband and wife and their friends in open court. But from your child's point of view this confidence may be unjustified. Court offices responsible for custody investigations are often understaffed, and their workers are not always adequately trained to find out what is best for children. Lacking both a professional basis for making judgments and legislative or judicial clarification of "best interests," the investigator may recommend as custodial parent the adult he himself would prefer. Though his report may tell the judge more about you and your child than he could otherwise find out, the observations it contains may be superficial, misleading, or irrelevant to your child's interest. Furthermore, such court ordered investigations, including evaluations by the child development experts who are sometimes called in for consultations, may be intrusive and disturbing to your child.

There are a number of ways you can assist the custody investigator and at the same time help your child. Remain calm and supportive. Try to avoid personality clashes and arguments. Cooperate with the investigator's requests for information and interviews, but do not hesitate to discuss with him how to minimize intrusion into your child's life. And explain to your child in a way that he can understand what is going on, in order to assuage the apprehension he may be feeling. It may be that in your case the custody investigation presents no problem because the investigator is a sensible and sensitive person and because your child is untroubled by what is going on. If, on the other hand, the experience is an unpleasant one, you and your child will have to accept the inevitable and make the best of it.

Expert Witnesses

Another source of information for the judge is the expert witness. Psychologists, psychiatrists, social workers, or other mental health professionals may be called by the lawyers for one or both parents, by the child's lawyer, or by the judge himself to render an opinion on which custody arrangement is in the child's best interest. This brings its own problems. A battle of experts is a frequent occurrence in courtrooms. While some divorcing mothers or fathers with sufficient funds might indeed shop around for an expert who comes out on their side, conflicting expert testimony is by no means always the result of experts' favoring the person who pays their fees. Rather, equally well trained, competent, and unbiased professionals may arrive at different recommendations depending on the philosophical or psychological stance from which they conduct their investigations and on how sharply and single-mindedly they focus on the custody issue from the child's perspective.

For instance, some child development experts are convinced on the basis of their training and clinical experience that although a continuous relationship with a loving adult who looks after his daily needs is important for a child's well-being, children are resilient enough to bounce back easily from separations and changes in relationships with their parents. They point to studies of children who have had such experiences that show that their learning skills are not adversely affected in the long run. And they believe that emotional upsets, partly because they are not reflected in a decline in learning skills, will be negligible and transient. They note that the child's regressive or difficult behavior which often follows the separation and divorce, such as a toddler's return to bed-wetting or thumb-sucking, an older child's difficulty in separating from his parents to go to school, or an adolescent's excessive rebelliousness or depression, is usually of brief duration. When making custody recommendations, experts of this school[2] are likely to stress personality traits and specific child-rearing skills of the competing parents.

Other child development experts[3] (whose views we share) believe that learning skills are not the only or even the most important measures of well-being and that resilience in this area does not necessarily have positive implications for a child's healthy emotional development. They believe that interruption of a continuous relationship with a loving and nurturing parent invariably leaves scars that do not heal completely and may affect the child's future ability to form relationships and become a good parent himself. Such experts are likely to recommend that the child stay with the parent to whom he has the stronger attachment (if they can determine which parent that is), even though the other parent may be better off, more intelligent, more consistent, more patient, and generally more appealing. And they are likely to recommend that custody determinations, once made, be final and not subject to change in the future on the basis of altered circumstances except in such extreme instances as child abuse or abandonment.

Nonexpert Testimony

In addition to the advice and testimony of mental health professionals, the judge may hear testimony from the parents and from nonexpert witnesses, such as neighbors, friends, and teachers, who have observed the child and his parents together. The difficulty here is that his judicial skill in determining a witness's truthfulness may be less helpful in custody cases than in other matters. This is because there are few absolute truths in parent-child relationships. Their intangible quality may not become clear to the judge through hearing what such witnesses say or observing how they say it. And too often witnesses will view these relationships through the eyes of one of the adults rather than through the eyes of the child.

Consulting the Child

In some states the law requires the judge to take the preference of a child over a certain age into consideration. Some judges like to interview the child privately in their chambers. Others are reluctant to do so, aware that they may lack the necessary skills to elicit his view. Alternatively or additionally, a judge may rely on the child's lawyer, if there is one, to inform him of the child's preference. Also, the child may be called as a witness in open court by one of his parents or by his own lawyer. But none of these ways of consulting a child necessarily result in the judge's making a wiser custody decision. Neither judges nor lawyers are generally qualified by training to know whether a child means what he says when he expresses a preference for a particular custody arrangement. Nor are they professionally qualified to interpret the behavior of a child too young to express his preference in words. And even if it is assumed that a judge, perhaps aided by a child development expert who is trained to understand and interpret a child's words and behavior, can accurately ascertain the child's preference, it is seldom in a child's interest to be asked to choose between his parents or to believe that his expression of preference will influence the judge's decision. Children often lack the maturity to make a wise choice. And choosing tends to create feelings of disloyalty toward one parent which can be quite devastating for the child as well as for the mother or father whom he "rejects." Indeed, this is why the law requires that the custody decision in the end be made by adults.

You may wish to weigh some of these considerations when you decide whether or not to use your child as a witness or to ask the judge to interview him. In the event that your child does have to testify in court or talk to the judge, you can help by assuring him that it is not disloyal to speak freely about you or to say with whom he prefers to live. And you can also tell the younger child that no matter what he says, the judge and not he himself will make the decision. This may not be true for older children. Depending on the law of the state and the judge's practice, the older child's preference may in fact be the chief or only determining factor in the custody decision. If this is so, it will be helpful for your child if you can assure him that you will continue to love him no matter whom he chooses.

A Court-appointed Lawyer for Your Child

Children, whose very existence depends on their parents, have a vital stake in the conduct and outcome of divorce proceedings. Recognition of this fact has led to the concept of giving children "party status" before the court, and this in turn has led to a growing trend toward separate lawyers for children. Some argue that children should be separately represented in all divorce proceedings; others, that independent counsel is necessary only if parents are in disagreement about custody or conditions of custody. We share the latter view because we believe that children are generally best off when their parents together make choices about their care and upbringing without outside interference, even in the context of divorce. But when parents are in conflict with each other about custody there are by definition at least two different views about what is best for the child, and an independent counsel may be necessary to represent the child's interest in a conflict-free way.

A court-appointed child's lawyer[4] may be charged either with making recommendations based on his own investigation of what is in his client's best interest or with representing the child in court as his advocate. In the latter case he may see his role as limited to finding out what the child wants, reporting it to the judge, and perhaps trying to get that preference implemented. But no matter what form his mandate takes, the job of the child's lawyer differs substantially from his usual role when representing an adult. Lawyers for adults know that they are to be guided by and should defer to what their clients tell them they want. But the child's lawyer may not be able to get definitive instructions from his client. Infants and very young children cannot say in words which custody arrangement they prefer, and older children may be too embarrassed, afraid, ashamed, upset, conflicted, or uncertain to say what they would like, especially since what most of them really want they cannot have—namely, a united mother and father. Also, lawyers are not specially trained or qualified to ascertain a child's preference. Further, even with older children it is by no means certain that what they say they want is truly what they prefer. For instance, a teenage girl might say that she wants to take turns living with her mother and father, not because that is what she would really like but because it is a way for her to avoid having to take sides between two people she loves and needs. And even if the lawyer has a pretty good idea what particular custody and visitation arrangement his child client would like, this is not necessarily what he should recommend to the judge (unless he sees his task as limited to being spokesman for the child's wishes), since what a child wants is not always—though it very often can be—what is best for him. Children's preferences may be taken into account to varying degrees, depending on their age, stage of development, and the particular state's laws. But they should not be burdened with making such a decision, both because they generally are not mature enough to exercise wise judgment and because it is not fair to force them to choose between their parents.

The court-appointed lawyer cannot turn to you, the child's mother and father, for instructions, since he was appointed precisely because the two of you were considered unable to represent your child in a conflict-free way in custody matters. But he can turn to you for help. Though you may disagree about which of you is to have custody or about visitation rights for the noncustodial parent, you can supply more information about your own child's needs, habits, customs, and relationships with the two of you than anyone else can. And you can help the lawyer to serve your child's interest not only by providing him with this information but by explaining his role to your child and encouraging the child to speak freely.

In addition to talking with you, the lawyer can and sometimes must make an independent investigation by talking to neighbors and teachers as well as to the child himself. Also, he can on his own initiative consult a child development expert to find out and inform him of the child's preference and the nature of his relationship to the two of you. He does his job well when he organizes informed inquiry and presents it to the judge.

Last but not least, the court-appointed child's lawyer can look to the statute that authorizes or mandates his appointment and to the judge who appoints him. For example, the law might require that the preference of a child fourteen years or older must be honored. If so, when a lawyer is representing a child of this age, his task will be limited to finding out what his client wants, and there will be no need for other investigations. Or the law might give preference to the parent who is more likely to provide continuity of affectionate care for the child; then the lawyer's efforts would be concentrated on finding out which parent that is, and he would not need to worry about other standards for determining who makes a better parent.[5]

You can help your child by discussing with his lawyer the possible disadvantages of extensive investigations. Talking with teachers and neighbors and even questioning the child himself are intrusions into the child's private life which ought to be kept to the minimum consistent with obtaining essential information. Thus, if one of you has looked after your child from birth without much help from the other—for whatever reason—it is unlikely that anything neighbors or teachers can say will help the lawyer make a wiser recommendation to the judge. And if the lawyer must ascertain your child's preference, you might suggest to him, especially if the child is very young, that he ask a child development expert to do this rather than interview the child himself. Above all, you might ask him to spare your child as much as possible from having to take sides between the two of you.

From your child's point of view, a court-appointed lawyer has drawbacks. Quite apart from the possible intrusiveness of his investigation, there is no certainty that his custody recommendation will serve your child well. Sometimes the lawyer does not devote sufficient time or care to his task or does not have the skill or sensitivity to do a good job. But even if this is not so—even if you and your spouse (or your respective lawyers) have agreed on a particular lawyer to represent your child and have submitted his name to the judge as a candidate for appointment by the court, and the judge has accepted your choice—a good result is not guaranteed.

Lacking, perhaps, a clear directive other than the vague "best interests" standard and faced with two different answers from the mother and father, there is the possibility that the lawyer will make custody recommendations based on his personal opinion of what makes a good parent. He may forget that when parents separate no alternative is ideal. Instead of looking for the best available solution he may put himself, or perhaps his own child, in the place of *your* child—his client—and ask himself, "Would I (or my child) like such a person as a parent?" He may recommend for or against a custodial parent for reasons that are quite irrelevant to your child's interest. For example, he might personally feel a distaste for obese people, bearded men, poorly educated people, people who live in communes, mothers who shout at or spank their children to discipline them, fathers who use foul language, people who do not appear on time for their appointments with lawyers, slovenly housekeepers, career-oriented women, men who do not earn a decent living, or vegetarians. He might think that reliable, well-educated, well-spoken, gentle, well-groomed women who have no desire to work outside the home make good mothers and that hard-working, sober men who are good disciplinarians make good fathers. Or he may think the opposite. He may not realize that none of these characteristics in a parent need have any significance for his client's well-being, and he may fail to concentrate on the crucial qualities of the preferred custodial parent—one with whom the child has primary bonds of love and trust which should not be broken and who has the ability to provide continued affectionate care for the child.

Another reason the recommendation of the lawyer may not work out well for your child is that it may be very difficult for him to keep his sympathy with or condemnation of the adult's divorce-related conduct from clouding his judgment about what is best for your child. He may feel very strongly, for instance, that a husband whose wife has abandoned him for another man ought not to lose his children as well, even though their stronger attachment is to their mother; or that a husband who has driven his wife to flee the home by his tight-fistedness and demeaning behavior should not have custody of their children, even though she has become so depressed as to be less able than the father to care for them as a single parent. Lawyers, like other professionals involved in child custody disputes, may sometimes forget that it is not in the child's interest to award custody to a parent as compensation for injuries suffered at the hands of his or her spouse.

Even when he avoids the pitfalls of being guided by his personal view of what makes a good parent and his sympathy for mother or father, the court-appointed child's lawyer may make a determination of "best interest" that does not meet your child's needs. In one case involving a visitation dispute—often a major point in contested custody cases—court-ordered visits were going badly. The ten-year-old child objected strenuously to visiting her noncustodial father and was clearly distressed, anxious, and unhappy; mother and father fought bitterly over each visit. The child's court-appointed lawyer recommended that the visits continue according to the court-ordered schedule. He reported to the judge that he had told the little girl how important it was that she see her father and had told her parents that they simply had to cooperate in making the visits successful. He concluded that what he characterized as "violent overreactions" on the part of child and parents made it obvious that the court ought to order professional counseling for all of them. This lawyer was confronted with the fact that visits by the noncustodial parent which he personally believed and which the law had presumed to be in the child's best interests were plainly not working out that way for this particular child. Because he concentrated on attaining an unrealistic ideal, he suggested that the obvious problems must be corrected by everyone's submitting to treatment rather than by changing the visitation order to accord with what the child could tolerate. It is difficult to see how this child benefited from having her own lawyer.

Even with the clearest instructions from the judge or the statute and the best-informed concentration on the interests of his client, your child's lawyer is not as likely to come up with a satisfactory resolution of custody issues as you, the mother and father—if you can only agree.

The Judge's Order Following a Contested Custody Hearing

The obstacles to focusing on and determining "best interest" do not mean that judges never succeed in doing just that. A good judge, aided by training and experience, may glean enough relevant information to make a wise custody order, especially where legislative mandate or case law precedent clarifies "best interests"—where, for instance, he is charged with protecting continuity of care and knows what to look for in determining who the "primary care-giver" is. The evidence may point overwhelmingly in one direction. But where the choice is not clearcut, where clues are complex and conflicting, the judge may defer to the opinions of others who often have less training, sensitivity, or insight than he himself possesses. Or he may disregard expert opinion altogether and fall back on his own instinct and personal preferences and prejudices. Or, faced with two equally suitable parents, he may decide that joint custody is the answer, even though one or both parents oppose it (or even, as has happened in at least one case, where neither spouse requested it)[6]— resulting in painful stress for the child. Further, by the time the judge finally reaches his decision, often after lengthy delays due to postponement requests by the lawyers, the various investigations, and heavy caseloads, the child may have suffered an intolerable period of uncertainty. And the judge's custody ruling may impose conditions that parents and children find very difficult to live with, such as a requirement that there be consultation with the noncustodial parent in a case where parents have never been able to agree on how to bring up their child, or that the custodial parent not move to another town or state without court approval. Orders such as these, though made in the name of protecting the child's relationship with both parents, may be self-defeating. When a child becomes a weapon in his parents' continuing war and can play mother and father off against each other, he is not likely to have a healthy relationship with either of them. If a custodial mother wants to move because she has found a better job elsewhere, because she has remarried and wants to move where her new husband lives, or for any other reason and must choose between sacrificing her plans and risking loss of custody, neither choice is likely to benefit the child.

In summary, it is generally better if the two of you (with or without the help of mediators or lawyers) can resolve your custody differences and do not force a judge to decide with whom your child should live and how often he should see his other parent. It will benefit your child if you can both focus on his needs—his strengths, weaknesses, and ties to each of you—and can refrain from using the threat of a custody fight as a bargaining chip to gain financial advantage, and from insisting on custody primarily out of spite. But even if your agreement is selfishly motivated, a judge would not necessarily make a better decision. Unseparated parents routinely make choices that accommodate the needs of one family member more directly than those of another. This does not mean that their children would be better off having courts rather than "selfish" parents make these choices. The same is generally true for children of divorcing parents; they do not benefit from having an impersonal judge make decisions which he cannot implement from day to day, but which the parents must implement and which they and their child must live with.

But perhaps the two of you simply cannot agree on custody. One of you may feel that the other and his or her lawyer are so powerful and coercive that you and your lawyer are likely to be browbeaten into agreeing to an arrangement that you know not to be in your child's interest. If you do need the judge to decide for you, it is better that he do so sooner than later, because your child needs to feel secure in his new situation as soon as possible. The younger he is, the more important it is that there not be long delays. For the same reason, your child will be better off if there are no temporary changes of care during the divorce proceedings, except in emergency situations, such as parental illness or child abuse. And, so long as the final outcome is uncertain, it is important that both of you continue to share parental responsibilities as much as possible or at least to see your child on a frequent and regular basis. This will make it easier for him to adjust to the custody decision no matter which of you is eventually designated by the judge to look after him.

Your child is likely to suffer under prolonged uncertainty and conflict. Therefore, once the judge has rendered his decision, you ought, if at all possible, to accept the situation as final even if your lawyer thinks there are grounds for appeal to a higher court, and you have sufficient funds to carry on a legal battle. And even though the custody award does not necessarily foreclose the possibility of future court intervention, especially because it is likely to contain directives not only on who should have custody but also on the rights and responsibilities of both parents,[7] for your child's sake you should not automatically avail yourselves of the opportunity to go back to court. The remaining chapters will focus on these and other matters in terms of what you can do to help your child live with your divorce.

PART III.
Living with the Divorce

8

The Shadow of the Law

Enforcing Provisions of the Divorce Decree

The judge's order contained in the divorce decree will award custody of your child to one of you or to both of you jointly and will specify the visitation rights and support obligations of the noncustodial parent. In some states, the order may even specify visitation rights of grandparents. By spelling out your legal rights and duties in relation to each other and to your child the decree underlines the fact that the law restricts as well as protects the freedom of action of divorced parents.

Whether the financial and custody provisions of the decree were agreed upon between you or were decided by a judge after a contested hearing, they are enforceable in a court of law. If your ex-husband fails to make obligatory support payments for your child, you can take him back to court; the judge can order him once again to make the payments, find him in contempt of court, and even send him to jail until he purges himself of contempt by bringing the payments up to date. If he has moved to another state, the Uniform Reciprocal Support Act provides the legal machinery for that state to process your claim against him. If your ex-wife does not permit you to see your child as ordered in the divorce decree, you can take her to court; the judge can admonish her to abide by the visitation order, find her in contempt of court, and even sentence her to jail. If she moves to another state, the courts of that state can, under the provisions of the Uniform Child Custody Jurisdiction Act, enforce the visitation provisions of the divorce decree at your request.

In practice, these legal remedies may be more illusory than real. It costs money to retain a lawyer to set the legal machinery in motion and have your day in court. The emotional cost can be high as well. The reopening of old wounds may cause you pain, and you may be concerned about the adverse effect of continued conflict on your child. And the tangible results of your seeking court enforcement may be unsatisfactory. If your ex-husband persists in not meeting his financial obligations either because he won't or because he can't, no amount of legal pressure will get the money to you. If your ex-wife consistently puts obstacles in the way of your seeing your child, you may become tired of hauling her into court; furthermore, the atmosphere between you and your child may become so poisoned by the continued battles that the visits become unrewarding for both of you. If your ex-husband fails to exercise his visitation rights, no matter how much you and your child want the visits, no court will or can make them take place. Generally, you can accomplish more by being civil to each other than by going back to court.

In spite of the difficulties of enforcement, the legal provisions of the decree can be significant. Respect for the law—or fear of punishment—may cause mother and father to abide by the judge's orders on custody, visitation, and support even if they would prefer not to. And in some eventualities the law can facilitate or hinder preferred conduct. For example, if a teenage girl whose mother has sole custody runs away to her father, the father

may be subject to arrest under some type of "custodial interference" law or even a kidnapping charge, unless he sends her back to her mother. If, on the other hand, mother and father have joint custody of their daughter, the father runs less risk of arrest or criminal prosecution if he decides to let her remain with him. Similarly, if a father who has long been delinquent in his court-ordered support payments suddenly comes into some money—perhaps by an inheritance or as a result of an insurance payment following an accident—his ex-wife can probably stake a legal claim against his newly acquired funds and prevent him from spending them if she acts quickly enough. This would be more difficult to accomplish if the decree had not spelled out his support obligations.

Changing Provisions of the Divorce Decree

Though some financial portions of the divorce decree may be final under the law, even in the absence of a separation agreement specifying finality,[1] this is usually not true for custody, visitation, and child support orders. State laws generally provide that mother or father can ask to have these orders changed if there has been a change in circumstances which was not contemplated at the time the decree was entered (unless mother and father have signed a separation agreement stipulating that its provisions are not to be altered, and the court has adopted this agreement, in which case it is more difficult to obtain a change).

What must be shown in order to obtain a modification varies from state to state and even from judge to judge. An unforeseen decrease or increase in either parent's income or unforeseen expenses for themselves or the child may lead to changes in the amount of court-ordered child support. Thus, if a noncustodial father has had to take a cut in pay or has had extraordinary medical expenses, the court might reduce his support obligations. On the other hand, if his income remains the same but he has remarried and is now supporting a new wife as well, the judge may not look kindly on his request for a reduction in payments to his former wife and child. Not only such drastic matters as child abuse or neglect but also a parent's prolonged illness, unconventional sexual habits, or even his or her moving to a different location might be legal grounds for obtaining a change of custody.

Because the standards for obtaining a change do vary from state to state, some dissatisfied parents have gone jurisdiction-shopping, taking themselves and sometimes their children to another state where they reopen custody dispositions in the hope of obtaining a more favorable ruling. In many cases conflicting custody decisions have been made about the same child in two or more states, because mother and father each went to court in a different state. The Uniform Child Custody Jurisdiction Act was designed to ease this problem. It spells out certain factors by which courts must be guided in determining whether or not they should assume jurisdiction in custody matters. However, the Act has not altogether eliminated jurisdiction-shopping because there are no hard-and-fast criteria for determining which is the appropriate state.

Protection against Parental Kidnapping

Neither the Uniform Child Custody Jurisdiction Act nor laws making it a crime to interfere with the custodial parent's relationship with the child are of much help if a parent simply snatches his child and then disappears without a trace, as some noncustodial parents have done. Some parents have kidnapped their children by snatching them from school or the street; others, by absconding with them instead of returning them to the custodial parent after a visit.

A parent who fears that his child may be kidnapped by his other parent has little legal protection. Courts are not easily persuaded to end a father's visitation rights because the mother alleges she fears he will not return the child but will disappear with him. Statutes and case law generally provide that visitation rights are not to be taken away except where serious harm to the child can be proved to have resulted from or to be likely to result from such visits. If a mother tells the judge she is afraid the father will kidnap the child and has in fact threatened to do so, the father may produce character witnesses to show that he is a reliable person who loves his child; he can deny having made the threat and claim that his ex-wife is viciously trying to destroy his relationship with his child. It is virtually impossible for a judge to determine who is speaking the truth in such cases, and, in the name of protecting the child's right to have contact with both mother and father, he is likely to uphold the father's right to visit. When they do occur, such kidnappings bring immense suffering and tragedy to individual children and their victimized mothers or fathers.

If you are afraid that your child will be kidnapped by your former spouse, your legal status as custodial parent does enable you to take some steps to protect yourself. If your child is in school, school authorities will honor your instructions that only persons specifically designated by you are to be allowed to fetch him. You can also ask the school to keep an eye out for your former spouse and suspicious strangers and inform you of their presence. If you think your former spouse may attempt to flee the country with your child you can write to the United States Passport Office requesting that no passport be issued for the child upon application of his other parent. In order for the passport office to honor your request, you will need to enclose a certified copy of the court order showing that you have legal custody.

You can also alert the local police to your fear, so that they will respond quickly to an emergency call from you. The police, too, may need to have a certified copy of the court order giving you custody; otherwise they may be unable to do anything to stop your former spouse, since in the absence of a custody order the law generally recognizes both parents as having equal rights to their children.

It should be emphasized that such precautionary measures should be taken only if they are less harmful than the emotionally charged climate they may create—only if you believe there is a real threat to your child's safety and the continuity of his care and relationships and not because you want to embarrass and hurt your former spouse. An atmosphere of fear and suspicion is not conducive to a happy childhood.

If a kidnapping does take place, you can enlist police help to find your child, though often the chance of success is not good. The Parental Kidnapping Prevention Act passed in 1980 is designed to provide federal assistance. It requires all state courts to abide by each other's custody decrees, instructs the FBI to help find parents who have snatched their children, and provides that the Federal Parent Locator Service can be used to help in the search. You might also enquire whether there is a private organization in your community that can help[2] and whether the news media is willing to be of assistance.

Protecting the Child's Relationship with Both Parents

The rules of law providing that custody decisions are not final and that the noncustodial parent's visitation rights are to be protected reflect the notion that although the granting of divorce marks the legal end of the husband-wife relationship, it does not end that of the child with his noncustodial parent. Nevertheless, with or without legal sanction, the child's relationships with both parents and especially with the noncustodial parent are bound to change significantly following the parents' separation and the entry of the divorce decree. The child is usually placed in the primary care of one or the other of his parents. Even when the custody award is "joint" one parent is likely to be the child's main care-giver. And even under those custody arrangements where both parents participate equally in the care and upbringing of their child, they do this no longer as part of one family but as individuals or as members of two different families.

The law may prohibit certain actions and may authorize or mandate others. But although legal rules may by their very existence influence and provide a framework for your child's postdivorce relationships with you, the law itself cannot create or safeguard them. Only you, his parents, can do that. In the remaining chapters we discuss, in turn, your roles as custodial and noncustodial parents, as parents in a joint custody situation, and, finally, as parents and stepparents in a new family.

9

If You Are the Custodial Parent

You and your child might not find it easy to be a single-parent family, especially at first. The more accustomed your child has been to having two parents at home, the stronger will be the impact of one parent's absence, and the greater will be the challenge for you to make his restructured life a good one. Your task is likely to be complicated by your own emotions. Do not be surprised if you feel angry not only at your spouse but also at your child. This may be because he reminds you both of his other parent and of the failure of your marriage.

In addition to the emotional wrench of the separation and divorce, there may be changes in material lifestyle. Perhaps you will need to economize—move to a smaller house or apartment, buy cheaper cuts of meat, enjoy fewer luxuries, and cut down on entertainment. If your child has been used to your staying at home and you are now pressed to take a job to make ends meet, this may be another unwelcome change for him. And even if you worked before your divorce, he may feel a difference now that his other parent is no longer available to him on an everyday basis.

Even if you do not need a job for financial reasons, you may want to work outside the home. You may find it difficult to respond to the incessant demands of a young child and miss the stimulation of adult company. It may be a strain for you to cope with the inevitable illnesses, upsets, and misbehavior if you have no one to share everyday worries. You need not and should not try to be a super-parent to compensate your child for your divorce. If you do not respect your own needs and comforts as well—including the needs to pursue your own career, make new friends, and find new interests—the quality of the care you give him is likely to suffer. You will tend to be more impatient, less willing to listen, more likely to lose your temper, and generally a less effective parent than if you have adequate time away from him. And you may also come to expect too much from your child, who instead of sympathizing with you makes you the target of his own fearful and angry feelings. A child will often direct his resentment at the parent he trusts more and with whom he feels safe, and that is usually the custodial parent.

You might find it useful to talk with others in similar circumstances about your concerns centering on your single-parent status and on your child's relationship with his other parent. Many communities have single-parent organizations which offer discussion groups, assistance in finding good day-care centers, and other services and social activities.

Care Arrangements for Infants and Toddlers

In order for your child to benefit from time spent away from you, the arrangements you make for his care should be appropriate for his age and responsive to his needs. It is important for your infant and toddler to be given individual attention and not to be looked after by different people each day. In order for a young child to thrive he must be able to form an emotional attachment to the person who takes care of his bodily needs, and this is impossible when that person keeps changing or looks after him in an impersonal, cold fashion. Perhaps you have a relative or friend who can be with your preschooler while you are out, or perhaps you can afford to hire a sitter. Or you may decide to enroll him in a day-care center. At his age it is more important for him to be with a caring adult who can give him some undivided attention than to have the company of other children. Therefore, try to find a day-care center whose workers do not have to spread themselves too thin and where the turnover in staff is not too great. Take time to talk with the person who is to look after your baby before you leave him there. It may help him to adjust to his new surroundings if his bedtime and feeding routines are as familiar as possible. You may want to bring his favorite toy, blanket, or pillow along. If he is used to being fed, burped, or played with in a certain way, it is helpful to show the worker how you do it. A good day-care center ought to be willing to listen to you and to comply with your requests as much as possible. If the person you talk to tells you that the center has its own way of doing things and there is no point in your providing any information about your baby, you should look elsewhere. Though some degree of uniformity may be necessary in order to run an efficient day-care center, there ought to be a willingness to adapt routines to the comfort and needs of the individual child.

Arrangements for School-age Children

If you have a school-age child, especially a young one, it is good if you can be at home when he comes back from school, even if he stays only long enough to say "Hi Mom" or "Hi Dad" before going out to play with his friends. It is important that he be able to touch base with you. If he has had a bad day, he may need you to comfort him. If he has done particularly well, he may want to come to you for praise and approval without waiting until evening. And sometimes he may just want to chat about nothing in particular, or not talk to you at all but know you are there if he should want you.

If you cannot be at home when your child returns from school, you may need to arrange for another adult to be there. It is not safe to leave a young child alone, and even adolescents may feel uncomfortable walking into an empty apartment or house. If you must leave your child alone, try to telephone home or at least leave a number where he can reach you. You know your own child and will surely sense when he is ready to be home alone after school and in the evening. There does come a time when your teenager is able to look after himself, resents a sitter, and treasures some time alone at home without you.

Financial Realities

While it would be unfair to burden your child with the details of your financial worries, it is equally unfair to him as well as to you if, when he is old enough to understand, you do not let him know your financial circumstances in general terms and have him share in whatever economies you must make. Depending of course on his age, you might want to explain, for instance, the need for fewer and less expensive clothes and presents or more meatless meals. You are not likely to do him any good if you exclude him from whatever economies are necessary. Do not think that because he has suffered from your divorce he must not be deprived of any material thing he asks for. Accepting financial realities and sharing in family economies is an important step on his road to maturity. If you habitually sacrifice your own needs and comforts to his, he will become aware of this sooner or later and may feel guilty or even angry at you for not being straightforward with him. Or he may, when he grows up, continue to expect and demand more than his share and find it difficult to be a responsible adult.

Your Child Needs His Childhood

It is important for your child to know what standards of behavior you expect from him. While you may expect and be tolerant of some rebellion or recurrence of outgrown childish behavior, you should not allow or encourage him to grow up wild and undisciplined. You cannot compensate for whatever he may have suffered because of your divorce by letting him do whatever he wants, any more than you can compensate with material goods. Even though he always seems to be pressing for greater freedom and fewer restrictions, he needs to know what the boundaries are. Otherwise he may become anxious and burdened by the need to set his own limits before he is mature enough to do so. Uncertainty as to what is expected of him will be added to the uncertainty caused by your divorce. Of course, the limits of tolerable behavior vary from family to family. Some parents are generally more permissive or stricter than others. Some place greater emphasis on cleanliness, punctuality at meals, good manners, or good school performance than others. What matters is that, whatever *your* standards are, you do not abandon them after your divorce either because you feel sorry for your child or because you are afraid your strictness will cause him to prefer your former spouse to you. And, so as not to let differences between parents in child-rearing styles become a source of conflict surrounding visitation, it will be best for your child if you respect his other parent's standards as far as is possible for you without going against what you believe to be important.

Necessary as it is for your child that you set standards of behavior and expect him to maintain them, it is equally important that you not burden him with excessive responsibility. Because you are a single parent you may need to rely on him more than you did before your divorce. He may have to do more for himself, for his younger brothers or sisters, and by way of household chores than would otherwise be the case. But what you expect from him ought not to exceed what is appropriate for his age. For instance, it might be tempting but it would be unwise for you, the father, to treat your oldest daughter more as a mother for your younger children than as your helper. Similarly, you, the mother, should not tell your son that he is now the man of the house. Premature responsibility can place a great burden on your child. He can do without comfort and luxury; he can be asked to help around the house and be somewhat independent sooner than he might like; but it is unfair to deprive him of his childhood.

Your Child's Visits with His Noncustodial Parent

It is best if you and your former spouse can work out visitation with respect for your child as well as for each other. Your child is not the one who got the divorce and should neither have to lose contact with one parent as a result of it nor be burdened, especially as he gets older, with an inflexible visitation schedule.

You, the custodial mother or father, may welcome the other parent's visits because you believe that they are good for your son or daughter and also because they may provide you with relief from your daily responsibilities and tasks. And your former spouse may love your child as much as you do and may want to spend enough time with him to maintain at least a semblance of their former relationship. If this is the situation, visits should go smoothly and the unsettling changes caused by the divorce may be minimized. It is even possible that the child will develop a closer relationship with the noncustodial parent. For instance, a visiting father might undertake more child care than before the divorce. He might learn to feed and diaper the baby, take the school-age child to birthday parties and baseball games, and discuss—or argue about—dating and world events with the teenager. Because time together is limited, he may make sure that it is uninterrupted and satisfying for both of them. If, however, the noncustodial mother or father is unable or unwilling to spend time with the child, no visits will take place. No one—including a judge—can force an unwilling parent to visit. You may have to comfort your child for his other parent's absence. You may need to assure him that the failure to visit is due not to his being unlovable but to circumstances beyond anyone's control, or even, if there is no other adequate explanation, to his absent parent's selfish, irresponsible, or unloving nature.

It might happen that your child balks at the visits. Perhaps he is becoming increasingly reluctant to cooperate with a court order to spend every Saturday with his noncustodial mother or father. The visits may interfere with his other activities or he may find them unpleasant because they seem to him like shuttling back and forth between two enemy camps. Or perhaps he is generally obstreperous and does not like to do as he is told. If you were not divorced you would be free either to insist that he do as you say or to be guided by his wishes. In the course of children's growing up parents constantly weigh when to make decisions for them and when to let them decide. But for a divorced custodial parent this prerogative is restricted. You may feel that your child is right not to want to visit or that at least the schedule should be changed to fit in with his other activities, but unless you can get your former spouse to agree, you may have to see to it that the visits take place. Unless there is evidence of physical or sexual abuse, courts almost always uphold the right of a noncustodial parent to visit his child, though they may experiment with different visitation arrangements to minimize difficulties. Thus, if you refuse to let the visits continue, your former husband or wife may take you to court to enforce visitation rights. Even if you are not taken to court, if you stop the visits, your alimony and child-support payments may be withheld, though legally there will probably not be a tie between support payments and visits. And if you try to get a court to enforce your former spouse's financial obligations, you might find the judge unsympathetic. You might argue that the failure of the visits is not your fault, that you have done your best to encourage them but that your child is upset for days before every visit and has nightmares afterwards and that, out of concern for his well-being, you cannot and will not force him to see his noncustodial parent. In spite of all this, you may be ordered to see that the visits resume, on the theory that since the child lives with you, you influence his attitude and behavior and that if the visits do not take place you have deprived him of the second parent to whom he is entitled. Some judges may act as if they believe that even coerced visits are worthwhile—at any rate, until children reach their teens. At that point even the most determined judge is likely to throw up his hands and admit that there is nothing he can do to help the noncustodial parent to maintain contact with an unwilling child.

Since the visits will take place even over your child's objections, you would be wise to persuade him to accept them and to try to work out more agreeable arrangements with your former spouse. You may have to lay down the law to your son or daughter, literally as well as figuratively, even though it is not a law that you have made and even though it may be one that is not to your liking.

Perhaps it is not your spouse but you yourself who opposes the visits. Perhaps your spouse deserted you for another partner and was able to get a no-fault divorce so that you did not even have the meager satisfaction of exposing his or her infidelity in court. It may seem to you that he or she is selfish and immoral and sets a bad example. But that may not be the way it appears to your child. He may love and need his other parent in spite of everything he or she did to hurt you. If you were to cut off the visits, your personal satisfaction would be attained at the cost of harming your child. Even adopted children who have never known their biological parents sometimes feel incomplete and become preoccupied with a search for their roots. Your child, who has known his other parent, may feel all the more cut off from a part of his life if he is forced to lose touch. For the same reason it may also be important for him to keep in contact with your former parents-in-law or other members of his absent father's or mother's family to whom he was close before the divorce.[1] By encouraging such continuity you can help to minimize the disruption of his accustomed life.

Another reason for you not to oppose visits is that if you did succeed in curtailing or preventing them your child might become anxious about what else you might do to him and his trust in you may be weakened. And in later years he may blame you for his having lost contact with his other parent. Thus your opposition to the visits might lead, paradoxically, to a weakening of his relationship with you, which would pose a further threat to his healthy development. Conversely, your support of reasonable visits would strengthen your child's trusting relationship with you.

Although you may have little control over whether and how often your child sees his noncustodial parent, there is much you can do to make the visits a successful and valuable experience. Try to put aside whatever bitterness and anger you may feel. Do not bad-mouth your former spouse to your child. If you can, emphasize his or her good qualities and, when speaking about your divorce, reminisce about the good times of your marriage as well. Help your child look forward to the visits by treating them as routine rather than as a dreaded duty which has been forced upon the two of you. It will be easier for him if you do not make him feel that this part of his life is a separate compartment from which you must be completely excluded and that it makes you unhappy if he enjoys the visits. But do not use him as a spy by asking him to report what is going on in what you consider to be enemy territory.

You should reconcile yourself to the fact that when visiting his other parent your child may be in a different environment than the one you might choose for him, and that this environment may well include the company of your former spouse's new sexual partner.

Be flexible about the visitation schedule so as not to invite repeated battles in or out of court. If you are asked to change a particular arrangement, try to be accommodating in hopes that your former spouse will be equally flexible in making changes to fit in with your and your child's plans. While you may be right to insist that the visiting parent not disappoint your child by failing to show up as promised, this does not mean that you should make a big fuss every time he is picked up or brought home a few minutes late.

Obviously, these observations and suggestions about what a custodial parent can do to make visits work in the child's interest are not based on specific knowledge and information about you and your family. They may not fit your situation. For example, they do not fit the case of one divorced mother who had custody of her six-year-old son and her eight-year-old daughter. The father lived only an hour's drive away, was remarried, and had an infant son with his new wife. The custodial mother maintained that visitation was destroying her family; the father, a teacher who had a good deal of free time late in the afternoons, was in the habit of dropping in without notice for short, informal visits. He also took the children home to his new family for long weekends twice each month. He seemed to enjoy having two families and felt it was important to stay in close touch with his two older children and for all three of his children to know each other. But the two children from his first marriage were unhappy and felt torn. The boy was uncomfortable with his father, and the girl disliked her weekend visits. The parents could not agree on how to improve the situation. Eventually this mother moved to another part of the country, hoping to find a calmer life for herself and her children far away from her ex-husband.

In the final analysis, you, the custodial parent, should not follow suggestions that simply do not work for you. And of course it is not only the custodial parent's attitude and conduct that affect the success or failure of the visits. In the next chapter we discuss, once again from a child's point of view, the role of the noncustodial parent.

10

If You Are the Noncustodial Parent

It's Not the Same as before Your Divorce

Your love for your child and his for you may be as great as ever. But although your relationship can be a good one, it cannot be the same as before your divorce. Your child, who has never stopped resenting the divorce, is likely to be angry with you, even if he denies this to you and perhaps even to himself. And, painful as it may be for both of you, at best you are now a visitor, albeit a regular and familiar one, and not an everyday parent.

It will help the child if you accept this gracefully and recognize that any undermining of his custodial parent's authority would further shake the security essential to his well-being. Therefore, you should try to work with rather than against your former spouse, even if you would do things differently if you were in charge. For example, if the custodial parent attaches great importance to regular meals and good table manners, do not say to your child that these don't matter. If the custodial parent is worried about tooth decay and insists on the child's brushing after every meal and not eating too much candy, don't stuff him with chocolate or let him skip brushing when he is with you. If the custodial parent has just refused to buy him a new bicycle because he has carelessly left the old one to rust outside in the rain, don't go out and buy a new one. You might be tempted to be less strict and more indulgent because you think this will make him love you more, and because it is perhaps harder to be strict and easier to be indulgent when you see him for only short periods of time. You might say that you and your former spouse are and always have been different people, and your child is used to this from the time you all lived together. But, though you cannot be expected to change your own personality and beliefs, you should not encourage your child to flout his custodial parent's authority. Even if your former spouse's standards are less rather than more rigorous than yours, nevertheless you should not make your child feel that they are wrong[1]—though you can ask him to conform to your standards while he is with you. He must and will learn that things are done differently in the two households. But his task of growing up will be complicated if he is confused about which parent is in charge. Like it or not, you must take a back seat. Otherwise, your child may tend, especially as he gets older, to play you and his other parent off against each other to get what he wants. By doing so he may obtain short term gratification, but at too great a cost, because he will miss out on the firm and consistent upbringing he needs to grow into a healthy and responsible adult.

Visits with Your Child

If you want to minimize disruption for your child you would be wise to start visits as soon after your separation as possible and to continue them with regularity. The younger he is, the harder it is for him to maintain a tie to you in your absence. Children under the age of three especially may quickly lose their feeling of attachment toward a parent whom they do not see every day. When you were still living together you may have noticed that your six-month-old infant cried bitterly when he was picked up by a visiting grandparent. He may show similar "stranger anxiety" toward you after only a few days' absence—what seems to you almost no time at all.

As your child gets older, try to be flexible about visits. If you have a visit scheduled when he wants to be with friends or go to a movie, or even when he wants to stay at home—for instance, to celebrate his stepparent's birthday—plan for another time instead. Remember what you liked to do when you were his age. As children grow older, their life naturally draws away from their parents, and children of divorced parents should not be hampered by rigid visitation demands. Similarly, you should not expect all your children, if you have more than one, always to visit together and spend their time with you in the same way.

You may perhaps have found it desirable or necessary to set up a detailed schedule of visits at the time of your divorce, precisely because you and your spouse were in conflict over their frequency or duration or about other matters pertaining to your child and you wanted to avoid acrimonious arguments over each visit. It is to be hoped, however, that your arrangement did not resemble the schedule agreed to by one divorcing couple and incorporated by the judge into their divorce decree. The mother had custody, and the father's "visitation" rights were as follows:

1. Vacation periods, not to exceed 14 days
2. One phone call a day
3. Consultation with the father and reports on nonschool activities
4. Father's participation in school conferences
5. Notification of medical emergencies and father's participation in decisions concerning child's needs

6. Father's obligation to pay college costs and right to participate in school selection
7. Visitation on:

Wednesday evenings
Alternate Saturdays and Sundays of each week
One weekend each month from 6:00 P.M. Friday to
    9:00 P.M. Sunday
Father's birthday and Father's Day
In alternating years, the child's birthday
In alternating years, the following holidays:

New Year's Eve and Day	Labor Eve and Day
Easter Eve and Day	Halloween Eve and Day
Memorial Eve and Day	Thanksgiving Eve and Day
Good Friday	Christmas Eve and Day
Independence Eve and Day[2]	

Sixteen months later, the mother petitioned the court to curtail the father's visitation rights, alleging that the child's emotional health had suffered. There could be little doubt, indeed, that for the child this setup was a nightmare. It sounds more like an arrangement made by two families for alternating use of a jointly owned vacation home or lawn mower than a plan for parental visits. The lifeless quality of the program took no account of the growing child's changing needs and interests. Such detailed advance planning would hardly be contemplated in any intact family, and it is unrealistic to assume that adhering to it would be in a child's interest when the parents are divorced. If your goal is for your child to benefit from and enjoy your visits, you should be prepared to depart from even the most carefully worked-out schedule if it becomes a burden to him.

Though you should adjust visits to your child's needs and interests, you should make every effort not to disappoint him by failing to show up when he expects you. It is important that he be able to trust the people he loves, and he can hardly continue to trust you if you are in the habit of letting him down.

You are more likely to keep up your visits if you can make them a pleasant experience for both of you. When you were living together, your time with and away from each other was probably a natural part of your daily lives. Now, when your time together is circumscribed and limited, it may have an element of artificiality which can prove to be a strain. Because your togetherness is more concentrated, you may be reluctant to intersperse your visits with activities from which your child would be excluded. But do not think that you must turn each and every visit into a special treat for him, regardless of what you yourself would enjoy doing. You don't have to take him to the zoo every Sunday if you find it a bore. Though you might want to plan activities that he particularly likes, you might also try to have him share your interests insofar as they are suitable for his age. Thus, he might accompany you on a shopping expedition or on a visit to a relative, or you might want to watch Sunday sports on television together. You may find that because you and your child miss each other, both of you look forward to the visits with unrealistic anticipation, and, like some longed-for holidays, they may prove disappointing. But frantic overactivity is likely to exacerbate rather than avert the resulting feeling of discontent.

Your visits with your child cannot be a good experience for him if his custodial parent fights them every step of the way. Therefore, try to work things out and be as accommodating as you can. If your child is supposed to be back by a certain time, do not habitually bring him home late. Do not use your visits either to cling to a remnant of your old relationship with your former spouse or to avenge yourself for a miserable marriage or for having been abandoned. Your child's bond with you is good for him only if it is not maintained at the expense of impairing his relationship with his custodial parent. He will suffer if you continue your conflicts or battles through him, or if you make him feel that "you can't love me if you love your other parent so much." Only when there is little or no conflict of loyalties can a child relate affectionately and in depth to each parent.

If, in spite of all your efforts to be fair and to work things out, your child does not want to see you, or your former spouse persistently opposes your visits, you may want to consider *not* going to court to enforce your rights or withholding alimony or support payments to put pressure on your former spouse, tempting as this may be. Much as you may feel your child needs you, if you can get to see him only by force of law and because his custodial parent is threatened with punishment, the child will suffer because he will be left without even one parent whom he knows to be in charge. Your court victory will be a hollow one. In the long run, your relationship will have a better chance if you remain in the background and hope that in time he will want to see you again or that your former spouse's opposition will soften. In the meantime, the best you can do for him is to assure him that, no matter how he and his other parent feel about you and about visits with you, you continue to love him and will be there when he needs you. Cutting down on support payments would serve him ill. His needs for food and shelter remain the same whether you get your visitation rights or not.

Asking for a Change of Custody

Though custody orders may not be final under the law, it is probably best if you accept the status quo and do not attempt to get custody yourself by claiming a "change of circumstances" unless your child has been subjected to abuse or neglect or unless your former spouse no longer wants to look after him. This is true whether you agreed at the time of the divorce that your spouse should have custody and have now changed your mind, or lost a custody battle in court. Your child needs continuity and security. Your divorce interrupted these, and it is important for his well-being that his new family situation not be disturbed by you, even if you think you would be the better parent. In your heart and mind the memory of the days when you lived together—when he ran to you for comfort and love—may be vivid, and you may think that you can restore that relationship with ease. But a child's sense of time is different from that of an adult, and his urgent need for daily loving care causes him to form strong emotional bonds with the parent who carries out that task. Your child probably experienced an emotional wrench when he was forced to separate from you at the time of your divorce. To separate him now from his custodial parent would be a second deprivation. The impact of this experience might be lessened but cannot be avoided by the fact that he once had equally close ties with you. You may think that he will quickly get used to living with you again. But each time he experiences separation from a care-giving parent, his sense of trust and security suffers a blow and his attachment to his new care-giver tends to become shallower. You may miss his daily companionship very badly. You may be deeply hurt as you see him drift away from you, perhaps because your former spouse makes it difficult for him to see you. You may think that you can provide more material comfort, better moral training, and greater intellectual stimulation than he is now getting. But if you are considering asking for a change of custody remember that what is best for you is not necessarily best for your child. From his point of view the advantages you have to offer may count but little when weighed against the detriment of a second uprooting. This may be very hard for you to accept because your love and feeling of closeness for him may be as strong as ever. But though time may have stood still for you in that respect, for your child it has moved on, and the changes that have taken place cannot easily be reversed. However, the adverse impact of changing custody is likely to be diminished the older your child was at the time of your separation, the more recent the separation, and the more you participated in his upbringing and care when you lived together.

You might be impelled to ask for a change of custody because you are convinced that your child wants to live with you. Perhaps he even tells you so. But it is not necessarily in his interest for you to abide by his wishes. All parents must at times decide whether to grant or deny their children's requests. Your divorce does not alter your child's need for parental control, although, just as would be the case if you were not divorced, your deference to his wishes is likely to increase with his age and maturity.

If you decide, for whatever reason, that a change of custody is necessary, try to persuade your former spouse to agree. Perhaps a consultation with a child development expert you both select might help you resolve your differences and focus squarely on your child's interest. A court battle should be the last resort because it is likely to increase your child's loyalty conflict and weaken his sense of security by impressing on him that it is not his parents but an impersonal judge who has control over his life.

11

Living with Joint Custody

It is generally best for a child if his parents rather than a stranger make decisions about his upbringing. Therefore, it is to be hoped that if the two of you at the time of your divorce agreed on joint custody the judge accepted it and incorporated it in the divorce decree even if he personally did not think it was good for your child. For the same reason, it is to be hoped that the judge did not impose joint custody over the opposition of one or both of you. Such a decision, though it might be motivated by the belief that what parents ought to do for their child's sake they can and will in fact do in obedience to a judge's order, is likely to exacerbate rather than mitigate parental conflict and the resulting harm to the child.

Even if you have freely chosen to continue to be jointly responsible for your child's care after your divorce, the success of the arrangement is not automatic. Much the same considerations are involved as apply to visits in the single-parent custody situation. Joint custody may fulfill its promise that your child will not lose a parent through your divorce if the two of you are on fairly friendly terms. It can even succeed if you hate and despise each other but are able to put aside your hostility sufficiently to cooperate in your child's care, to avoid making him a battlefield for your wars, and, equally important, to resist the temptation to get him to take sides between you. He may then be able to relate to both of you in a positive way; to experience a minimum of disruption in his life as a result of your separation and divorce; to feel that he still has two parents, neither one of whom has given him up or deserted him; and to have the advantage of both male and female guidance. If, on the other hand, your child is involved in continuing conflict between the two of you, he is likely to suffer from being torn by irreconcilable loyalties, from inconsistent parenting, and from persistent turmoil.[1] Rather than feel that he has two whole parents, he may experience his situation as having two inadequate half-parents.

The success of joint custody will require continued effort on your part. For instance, you might have to consider making changes (or refraining from making changes) in your personal life in order to accommodate your child's needs. Thus, you might decide to stay at home more in the evenings and on weekends while your child is with you instead of going out. Or, if you have the opportunity for a better job in a different town or state, you might consider whether to forego the promotion because the move would make joint custody unworkable and deprive your child of its benefits. Above all, you must be ever mindful that your child's development may require changes in a hitherto satisfactory arrangement. There may have been no problems with your preschooler's being cared for on alternate days by each of you; but this does not mean that the arrangement will necessarily suit him once he goes to school. It may become difficult for him to move from the house or apartment of one parent to that of the other carrying schoolbooks and other belongings with him. And, depending on how far away from each other you live, such moves may interfere with his after-school activities like visits to class-mates or taking part in neighborhood ball games.

Joint custody can continue to be in your child's interest only if you look at it consistently from his point of view. For instance, in the early days of your divorce your child may have spent weekends and holidays with you and school days with his other parent. You may have given up much of your social life in order to devote yourself to him. You may be quite hurt and disappointed to find that as he grows older he usually has plans for Saturdays and Sundays that involve friends of his own age and exclude you. That is a natural development, and you should be prepared to accept it and not expect to be repaid for your former sacrifice.

If you have several children, an arrangement that suits one of them may not suit another. While it is generally preferable for brothers and sisters not to be separated by their parents' divorce, it does not follow that in a smoothly working joint custody situation (any more than with respect to visits) all the children must spend the same day or parts of days with the same parent in the same manner. This is not the way it is for children whose parents live together; older and younger brothers and sisters do not have the same activities, and it would place an unwarranted burden on children of divorced parents if joint custody were to hamper their normal freedom to pursue their separate interests.

It may happen that, quite apart from changes necessitated by your child's growing older, your joint custody arrangement is or becomes unsatisfactory because one or both of you is unable or unwilling to cooperate with the other. Conflicts may have arisen with respect to religious training, education, discipline, money, bedtimes, or attitudes toward sexual behavior (yours or the child's); or one of you may have decided to move to a distant place. Whatever the cause of the trouble, it may necessitate chang-ing the arrangement or even abandoning the idea of joint care and responsibility for your child. For the same reason that joint custody would not have been a good choice for your child if one of you opposed it at the time of your divorce, it cannot continue to work in his interest when such opposition develops and persists over time.

Again, it will be best if you can resolve the difficulty between yourselves. Going back to court should be the last resort, both because it does your child no good to be fought over and subjected to the acrimony of a court battle and because a judge is less likely than you, the parents, to find a solution which is best for your child and which all of you can tolerate. A judge might rule either that joint custody should continue or that the parent who wants to end it automatically loses custody. But, just as one spouse's "fault" for the failure of a marriage ought not to be the primary reason for awarding custody to the other, it would not serve your child's interest if sole custody were to be given automatically to the parent who is "innocent" of the failure of joint custody. For instance, if your child is less close to you, his father, than to his mother, and if his mother decides to move to another part of the country either because she found a good job or to escape from what she claims to be your constant interference, it may be that your child should be placed in her sole custody even though in your eyes she was wrong to move.

If you focus on your child's interest rather than on what seems fair to the adults, this should facilitate your finding a sensible and mutually acceptable alternative to an arrangement that no longer works. That is what happened in the case of one divorced couple who had initially agreed to joint custody for their four-year-old daughter. The father was a physician. The mother had resumed medical training and was now in her senior year. They lived in apartments one block apart. The original arrangement was that their daughter would stay with her mother Monday to Friday and with her father on weekends. The little girl attended a day-care center during the week. Disagreements arose because the father was now living with another woman who had two children of her own from a previous marriage—boys aged five and eight. The mother was worried about the little girl's staying with her father in this altered situation. The father countered by suggesting that his daughter live with him and his woman friend all the time, since the woman worked only a few hours a day and had time to look after the child, whereas the mother was now extremely busy preparing for final examinations. Indeed, some time ago she had asked the father to change the arrangement so that the little girl would spend weekdays with him and weekends with her. Both parents had found their previous court experience unsatisfactory and were willing not to seek enforcement of their legal rights under the divorce decree. Instead, with the help of a child development expert, they sought to find a new arrangement based on what best suited the little girl rather than on whose fault it was that the original joint custody plan no longer worked.

Joint custody is likely to benefit your child if the two of you are willing and able to be open to change, to be sensitive to the child's point of view and his changing needs, to talk with each other, and to consult your child, if he is old enough, about his wishes and difficulties. When such give-and-take and flexibility exist, joint custody may approximate the parent-child relationship in an intact family. But to say this is also to state one of the difficulties with joint custody—namely, that in one way it denies the reality of your divorce. This reality may intrude especially when one of the parents forms a new relationship. The impact of this on your child is discussed in the next chapter.

12

Stepfamilies

New Relationships

When parents begin to see new adult partners after their separation, they can evoke conflicting emotions and responses in their child. His reactions may reflect simultaneously the wish for the return of the absent parent, the need to replace him, and the fear of losing the remaining parent's affection.

You, the mother, might find to your embarrassment that your two-year-old daughter behaves very lovingly toward even casual male visitors, or that your ten-year-old son is unaccountably rude to the man you are dating. You can be alert not to arouse your children's hopes or fears prematurely. You might explain to your son that you have no immediate intention of marrying again and that you may be going out with several different men for a while—if this is the true state of affairs. To your little girl, words may not mean much, but you and your man friend might avoid hugging and kissing in her presence. If and when you decide to live together, you may want to consider that the more time he spends with you and the more he acts like a husband and father, the more likely it is that your children will become attached to him and the more difficult and confusing it may be for them if he should leave. If such experiences are repeated their confusion will deepen, and it may become more difficult for them to trust and love those around them.

Remarriage

A parent's remarriage is another big change in the life of the child—often for the better. He will benefit if the new family is happy and united and if he can feel that he has a secure and loving place in it. On the other hand, if his stepparent is unloving and abusive, or if the new marriage turns sour, he is likely to suffer. But even if his stepparent is all that can be desired and everyone around him is happy, his adjustment will not necessarily be smooth.

A child's fantasy of seeing his parents reunited receives a blow when one of them remarries. This may help to account for some annoying behavior. For instance, if you, the mother, have remarried you may find that the same little girl who behaved so affectionately to her future stepfather when he first came to your home—perhaps called him "Daddy" and climbed into his lap—may act sullen and unhappy after you have married him. And your ten-year-old son may continue to be rude. The children may rebuff your new husband's overtures of friendship and affection and generally make life very difficult for you. What their behavior may mean is that they miss and want a father but at the same time are distressed by a stranger's taking their own father's place.[1]

The impact on a child of his parent's remarriage is not limited to his initial emotional reaction. Not only does he have to get used to a stepparent, but his relationship with both of his own parents, as well as other circumstances of his life, may change.[2] For example, a child's remarried custodial mother may now have a name that is different from his. She may move to a different area to be with her new husband. For the child this means a new school, a parting from old friends, and a need to make new ones. The mother may be preoccupied with making the marriage work and have less energy or time for him. A remarried noncustodial father might make fewer visits or reduce support payments because of emotional and financial demands made by his new family. The parent who has not remarried may resent the new marriage, and as a result problems may arise over visitation. For instance, a custodial mother might put obstacles in the way of the remarried father's visit when the occasion is an outing to celebrate the stepmother's birthday. A noncustodial father might make greater demands for visits and be unduly rigid in enforcing a visitation schedule after his former wife remarries. Or he might reduce his visits or stop them altogether, either because the child now lives too far away or because he feels hurt that the stepfather has usurped his place. He might be tempted to cut down on child support payments because he thinks that the man who has taken his place as husband and father ought to assume his financial responsibilities as well.

If you focus on your child's well-being when you or your former spouse remarry, you can minimize such unsettling changes and help him benefit from the new situation. For instance, if you are a custodial parent who has remarried and moved to another home, you might try to keep your child's room arrangement the same as before; perhaps he can keep his own bed and bedspread. If at all possible, do not make the move an occasion to throw out his old toys or other belongings. Try to let him see his friends from the old neighborhood.[3] If possible, spend some time with him alone in the same way you did before your remarriage. Above all, show him by your behavior that your new family does not diminish your love for him. If you are a noncustodial parent who has remarried, try to see your child as much as he would like and is used to, and do not neglect him emotionally or financially for your new family.

If it is your former spouse who has remarried, do not let whatever jealousy or anger you feel spill over onto your child. If he lives with you, do not make it more difficult for him to visit his other parent and stepparent. If he does not live with you, be as available to him as he wants, but do not use your visits to burden his life with his new family. Allowing him to feel all right about his relationship to his stepparent will enhance not diminish his tie to you.

Your child will do best if you respect his need for continuity and security—if you allow and encourage him to become part of a new family without feeling disloyal and without losing the love and companionship of a parent he loves.

Other Children in the New Family

Often when mother or father remarries, the child is also confronted with new brothers and sisters—a ready-made new family. Again, this may invoke mixed feelings. A little boy may be jealous of the attention paid to an older boy by his remarried mother, who is trying to cement her relationship with her stepson. Later he may come to enjoy the companionship of his stepbrother. A little girl whose father has remarried may enjoy playing with her baby stepsister but be angry at having to share her father's attention with another child. If the stepbrother or stepsister is of the same age, the child's sense of rivalry may be all the more pronounced. And if there are several children in the stepfamily, the child may be overwhelmed. He may feel like an outsider and become depressed. At the same time, he may tend to be more possessive of his own mother or father.

When a parent and a stepparent have a new baby together, it may happen that a child who had apparently settled down and become comfortable with his new family becomes angry, resentful, withdrawn, or disobedient, or lapses into childish behavior. Almost everyone is familiar with the jealousy aroused in a child by the arrival of a new brother or sister. This jealousy may be especially strong in the case of half-siblings, whether it is the child's custodial or noncustodial parent who has the baby. The baby may seem to belong to the child's father or mother more completely than he himself does. And its arrival may also make his dream of reuniting his parents—a dream that may have persisted in spite of the remarriage—even more unattainable.

As with other changes accompanying and following the parental separation, your child will do best if you are alert to how he is likely to experience these events and continue to assure him of a secure and loving place in the family.

13

Conclusion

Children depend on their parents for life, nourishment, and guidance. Because they are not adults capable of making adult choices, they can have little or no effective say in their parents' divorce and its aftermath, even with respect to arrangements for their own care. But they have feelings about these matters. Though legislators, lawyers, judges, and child experts can make life harder or easier for these children by their decisions and actions, it is the parents who are best qualified to make and implement the choices that affect all their lives. Separating parents may look to others for help and guidance; laws and judges may make rules or provide guidelines; but such help, laws, rules, and guidelines are beneficial to children only to the extent that they are accepted, agreed to, and acted upon by their parents.

If you can get yourself into the frame of mind of asking which of you is more likely to be able to meet your child's day-to-day needs or, to put this in another way, which of you should be awarded to your child rather than which of you deserves to be awarded his custody—if before, during, and after your separation, divorce, and remarriage you can look at these events through his eyes and respect his basic needs for love, security, continuity, and consistency—you will have taken a long step toward serving his well-being and, in the long run, yours as well.

Notes

NOTES TO CHAPTER 1

1. These figures are taken from National Center for Health Statistics reports for 1974, 1976, and 1977. In 1981, according to the Census Bureau, 20 percent of all children under eighteen lived in one-parent families (see 8 *Family Law Reporter* 2628). In the same year, according to provisional data from the National Center for Health Statistics, 2,438,000 marriages occurred and an estimated 1,219,000 divorces were granted. Lenore J. Weitzman, "The Economics of Divorce: Social and Economic Consequences of Property, Alimony, and Child Support Awards," 28 *UCLA Law Review* 1181 (1981).

2. "Sometimes a child of divorced parents stops talking to anyone and withdraws into herself because she feels at home nowhere. And they want the child treated for that as if it were an illness and not a misfortune" (comment made to the authors by Anna Freud).

3. You may wish to share your concerns about your separation and divorce with another adult and to seek advice, not only to help you through this difficult time, but also to sensitize yourself to what it means to your child, so that you can take this into account as you go about restructuring your life. If you are worried about your child's reactions or behavior, such as sleeping or eating disturbances, your pediatrician may be able to provide advice and reassurance. Your

community might have a single parents' group or a support group for noncustodial mothers or fathers whose members have had experiences similar to yours and can give you sympathy and understanding, as well as practical suggestions on how to cope. Or you might prefer to speak with a professional counselor—a qualified stranger in whom you find it easier to confide. You need not be embarrassed or ashamed if you cannot manage alone. Seeking help if you need it can be a sign of strength, not of weakness. See also chapter 5 for a discussion of counseling in relation to resolving disagreement about custody.

4. See Joseph Goldstein, Anna Freud, and Albert J. Solnit, *Beyond the Best Interests of the Child,* rev. ed. with epilogue (New York: Free Press, 1979).

5. "His or her" and "he or she" make for clumsy writing and annoying reading. Therefore, we generally use masculine pronouns when referring to a child, but, unless apparent from the context, the discussion applies equally to boys and girls. And when we use "child" in the singular, the comments are generally meant to apply no matter how many children there are in the family. For the same reason, we refer to all professionals with masculine pronouns.

NOTES TO CHAPTER 2

1. Goldstein, Freud, and Solnit, *Beyond the Best Interests of the Child,* pp. 13–14. Reprinted by permission of the publisher. Copyright 1979 by The Free Press.

2. See, e.g., John Bowlby, *Maternal Care and Mental Health,* World Health Organization Monograph no.2 (Geneva, 1951); Margaret Ribble, *The Rights of Infants* (New York: Columbia University Press, 1943); Sally Provence and Rose C. Lipton, *Infants in Institutions* (New York: International Universities Press, 1962); Anna Freud and Dorothy Burlingham, *Infants Without Families: Reports on the Hampstead Nurseries,* vol. 3 of *The Writings of Anna Freud* (New York: International Universities Press, 1973).

3. *Quilloin v. Walcott,* 434 U.S. 246, 255 (1978).

NOTES TO CHAPTER 3

1. Goldstein, Freud, and Solnit, *Beyond the Best Interests of the Child,* pp. 13–14. See also above, chapter 2.

NOTES TO CHAPTER 4

1. See chapter 3, above, for a discussion of the child's tendency to blame himself for his parents' divorce.

NOTES TO CHAPTER 5

1. See, e.g., H. J. Folberg and M. N. Graham, "Joint Custody of Children Following Divorce," 12 *University of California–Davis Law Review* 522 (1979); Ciji Ware, *Sharing Parenthood after Divorce: an Enlightened Custody Guide for Mothers, Fathers, and Kids* (New York: Viking, 1982); Group for the Advancement of Psychiatry, Committee on the Family, *Divorce, Child Custody, and the Family,* GAP Publications, vol. 10, no. 106 (New York: Mental Health Materials Center, 1980).

2. One child who alternated his residence weekly between the homes of each of his parents, according to the testimony of a teacher" never refers to his home. He refers to his daddy's home and his mommy's home." *Faria v. Faria,* 38 Conn. Supp. 37, 42–43 (1983).

3. This was apparently one California family's solution. See "Splitting up the Family," *Newsweek,* 19 January 1983, 43.

4. In some cases, judges have automatically denied custody to the parent who wishes to terminate joint custody.

5. For an optimistic view of mediation from a practitioner, see John N. Haynes, *Divorce Mediation—A Practical Guide for Therapists and Counselors* (New York: Springer, 1981).

6. Though mediation (sometimes called "conciliation,") is a prerequisite in some states to getting a divorce, this process is designed not to prevent divorce but to minimize the bitterness of contested custody or property dispositions.

NOTES TO CHAPTER 6

1. You yourself may find the name listed in the telephone directory or get the information from a local child guidance, family counseling, or women's center.

2. In an Illinois case Russian immigrant parents wishing to return to the USSR were initially prevented from taking their teenage son with them when he and other family members objected. Later, however, the Illinois Supreme Court ruled that the parents could take their son but would have to return from the Soviet Union in person to pick him up. The initial restriction was based on the argument that normal parental rights and authority were outweighed by the damage to the child that would result from his being forced to live in a totalitarian society.

NOTES TO CHAPTER 7

1. Some judges, legislators, and lawyers believe that judges should carefully scrutinize separation agreements presented to them and alter them if they think that the child's interest has been sacrificed to other considerations. We disagree. A judge, no matter how well motivated, can't learn enough about a particular child to guarantee a better result—especially when at least one of the parents opposes his decision.

2. See, e.g., Michael Rutter, *Maternal Deprivation Reassessed* (Middlesex, England: Penguin Books, 1972); Ann M. Clarke and A. C. B. Clarke, *Early Experience: Myth and Evidence* (New York: Free Press, 1976); Jerome Kagan, Richard B. Kearsley, and Philip P. Zelazo, *Infancy: Its Place in Human Development* (Cambridge: Harvard University Press, 1978).

3. See, e.g., Bowlby, *Maternal Care and Mental Health*; S. Ritvo and A. J. Solnit, "Influence of Early Mother-Child Interaction on Identification Processes," *Psychoanalytic Study of the Child* 13:68–85 (New York: International Universities Press, 1958); Anna Freud, *Normality and Pathology in Childhood,* vol. 6 of *The Writings of Anna Freud* (New York: International Universities Press, 1969).

4. Some states provide for the appointment of a guardian-ad-litem—a

law guardian. Such a person, who need not be a lawyer and may in fact himself decide to retain a lawyer to represent the child in court, is asked to speak for the child and represent his interests because the child, as a minor, is considered "incompetent" before the law.

5. Assuming, of course, that there are no overriding factors such as child abuse or disabling illness present in the case.

6. *Beck v. Beck,* 432 A. 2d 63 (1981). The New Jersey Supreme Court, though it sent the case back for a new hearing to the trial court that had made the joint custody order because of a possible change of facts and relationships since the order was made, nevertheless affirmed the right of trial judges under certain circumstances to order joint custody even though neither parent requests it. See also *Strohmeyer v. Strohmeyer,* 183 Conn. 353 (1981), where the Connecticut Supreme Court seemed to suggest that a trial court has this right, provided it holds a hearing first.

7. Of course, parents can at any time change court-ordered custody arrangements simply by agreeing on another arrangement.

NOTES TO CHAPTER 8

1. In some states, for example, if the divorce decree does not provide for alimony, it is unobtainable at a later time.

2. One such organization, Child Find, headquartered in New Paltz, N.Y., describes itself as "An International Network for Locating Missing Children."

NOTES TO CHAPTER 9

1. However, legally mandated, court-enforceable grandparent visitation rights are not in a child's interest, because they interfere with what the child needs more—a parent who is in full charge.

NOTES TO CHAPTER 10

1. There are, of course, exceptions. If your former spouse tells your child to steal or cheat in school, for example, you would be well advised to tell your child this is wrong.

2. *In re Marriage of Solomon,* 84 Ill. App. 3d 901 (1980) at p. 902.

NOTES TO CHAPTER 11

1. Many courts recognize this. See e.g., *Seymour v. Seymour,* 180 Conn. 705 (1980): "the two parents exhibited marked and irreconcilable differences in their personalities, in their life-styles, and in their child care practices. The father was characterized as orderly, well organized, responsible and inflexible, while the mother was described as energetic, impulsive, immature and open. These disparities in the parents' personal orientations led to opposing viewpoints with respect to the child's diet, health-care and daily living arrangements and hence to the breakdown of joint custody of the child" (at p. 708).

NOTES TO CHAPTER 12

1. "When I think of a stepparent I think of someone mean and someone who doesn't love you as much as your own parents. But I know that isn't true. All I know is that I want my own mom and dad." The comment of a nine-year-old girl quoted in "When a Parent Remarries," *New York Times,* 3 January 1983.
2. The following letter to Ann Landers illustrates that the changed circumstances caused by remarriage can result in bewildering situations for adults as well as for children:

Dear Ann Landers: I am John's third wife and I need to know what is proper under the circumstances. John's daughter (by his first wife) is getting married in the spring. Missy (not her real name) has asked her father to give her away.

Missy's mother (wife No. 1) will also be attending. Missy has asked her father's second wife (wife No. 2) to be her matron of honor. My question is about the seating arrangements for the dinner. There will be a head table. So, where should I sit? Do I belong next to my husband at the head table, or with the other guests? Also, what about the formal wedding pictures? Will you please tell me who should be included in the photos? (P.S. We all get along very well. No problems.)—Win, Place and Show.

Dear Show: People ask me if my mail has changed in the last 26 years. Your letter is an excellent example of one of the major changes.

Wife No. 2 (the matron of honor) should be seated with the wedding party, next to the best man. You, wife No. 3, should sit with the guests. If wife No. 1 or wife No. 2 has remarried, you could sit with one of the husbands or between the two.

As for the formal wedding photos, only the members of the wedding party should be included. These days, if all the exes and their spouses were included it would require a camera with an extra-wide lens.

From the *New Haven Register*, 10 January 1982; reprinted by permission of Ann Landers and the Field Newspaper Syndicate. Copyright 1982 by Field Newspaper Syndicate.

3. The idea of helping your child to maintain as much continuity as possible with his friends and surroundings is of course not limited to remarriage but applies throughout the separation and divorce.

Glossary

Words and phrases (some of which but not all are used in this book) that divorcing parents are likely to encounter when dealing with lawyers, judges, and mental health professionals.

Alimony. Court-ordered payments from one spouse to the other during or after divorce proceedings.

Alimony pendente lite or *interim alimony.* Alimony payments ordered to be made while the divorce is pending but before the final decree.

Alternating custody. Usually means that physical as well as legal custody of the child is alternated by the parents. See also *Divided custody, Joint custody, Shared custody.*

Appellant. A person who appeals the decision of one court to a higher court.

Appellee. A person in whose favor a court has made the decision from which the appellant has taken an appeal.

Child development expert. A child psychiatrist, child psychoanalyst, child psychologist, educator, pediatrician, or social worker.

Child psychologist, child psychiatrist, or *child psychoanalyst.* Members of their respective professions with special training in understanding both what children need and what they feel and say. See also *Child development expert, Psychiatrist, Psychoanalyst, Psychologist.*

Child's attorney. A lawyer appointed to represent the child's interests in divorce proceedings. The way in which the child's attorney perceives his role may vary from state to state and even from attorney to attorney. See also *Guardian-ad-litem.*

Child support. Payments ordered by the court to be made by a spouse for the support of the divorcing couple's minor children. Even though these payments are generally made to the spouse who has custody, they are separate from alimony and continue even if the custodial parent remarries.

Child support pendente lite or *interim child support.* Child support payments ordered to be made while the divorce is pending but before the final decree.

Cohabitation. A term sometimes used in statutes or by lawyers and judges to describe a divorced spouse's living with another person as husband and wife without getting married.

Conciliation. See *Mediation.*

Contempt citation. A court's finding that one parent is in violation of a court order. This is meant to persuade the "contemptuous" party to comply with the order. If he does not, he may be sent to jail by the judge until "purged" of contempt by promising to obey the order (allowing visits by the other parent or making overdue support or alimony payments, for example).

Contested matter. A case in which the spouses have been unable to agree on one or more issues such as custody, visitation, alimony, or child support, and the judge must decide on the basis of what he learns from witnesses at a court hearing.

Counsel. Another name for a lawyer.

Counseling. Giving advice to a person who is having difficulties in his life. A professional counselor may have been trained initially as an educator, psychiatrist, psychologist, social worker, priest, minister, or rabbi. Lawyers are generally not trained to do counseling.

Custodial parent. In the legal setting, the parent who is given the right and responsibility for looking after the child. A divorce decree usually contains an award of custody and also describes the rights, if any, of the noncustodial parent and the consequent limitations of the custodial parent's rights. Under certain circumstances, courts can change custody orders at the request of one parent.

Custody. The right and duty of caring for a child.

Custody pendente lite or *interim custody.* Custody award made while a divorce is pending; not necessarily the same as the "final" custody award in the divorce decree.

Defendant. A person who is taken to court by another person.

Dissolution of marriage. Another name for divorce, used in some jurisdictions.

Divided custody. Refers either to an arrangement in which the child divides his time between mother and father or to one in which some children in the family are awarded to one parent and some to the other. See also *Alternating custody, Joint custody, Shared custody, Split custody.*

Equitable distribution. A rule adopted in a number of states for making property settlements on the basis of where the assets originally came from, taking into account the earnings of husband and wife during the marriage as well as uncompensated work such as keeping house and rearing children.

Guardian-ad-litem. A person, not necessarily a lawyer, whose appointment is required by some state laws. His task is to represent the child's interests in contested custody matters. See also *Child's attorney.*

Irretrievable breakdown. See *No-fault divorce.*

Joint custody. A variety of arrangements by which legally separated or divorced parents share in looking after their child or making decisions for him. Sometimes a distinction is made between "physical" joint custody, meaning that the day-to-day care of the child is divided between the parents, and "legal" joint custody, meaning that the child lives with one parent most of the time but the other parent is involved in decision-making. Or it can mean that both physical custody and decision-making are the sole prerogative of each parent in turn for specified periods of time. See also *Alternating custody, Divided custody, Shared custody.*

Judge. A person, usually a lawyer, who has been elected or appointed to perform judicial functions, that is, to render decisions in court cases.

Jurisdiction. The legal power of the court of a particular state to hear a case. The laws of a particular state are sometimes referred to as the laws of that "jurisdiction."

Legal separation. A procedure in some states whereby couples can legally separate and court orders can be made for custody, alimony, and child support. In effect it may resemble a divorce except that the spouses are not free to remarry.

Lump sum alimony. Alimony payments that are fixed in amount and not related to a time period or terminated by remarriage of the recipient or some other event.

Mediation. A method of trying to resolve disputes in a nonadversarial setting. One person or a team discusses the issues with the disputing parties and tries to help them work out a solution that is acceptable to both of them.

Modification of an order. A change in the court order pertaining to custody or financial matters following a petition by one of the parents.

No-fault divorce. A divorce that may be obtained without either spouse's having to show that the other has, for instance, committed adultery, or been physically or mentally cruel to the other. To get a no-fault divorce it is enough that the marriage has broken down and there is no hope of reconciliation—that there has been an "irretrievable breakdown."

Noncustodial parent. The parent who is not awarded custody. Generally he or she is given visitation rights and often some decision-making rights as well.

Periodic alimony. Alimony payments that continue for a specified number of years, or until the remarriage of the recipient spouse or some other specified event. If none of these contingencies occur, alimony payments continue (unless modified by court order) until the death of the paying spouse.

Petitioner. See *Plaintiff.*

Plaintiff. The person who commences a particular proceeding in court.

Primary caretaker or *primary caregiver.* The person (usually but not always a biological parent) who does most of the day-to-day caring for and looking after the child.

Primary psychological parent. The parent with whom the child has the stronger bonds. See also *Psychological parent.*

Property settlement or *assignment of property.* A court order transferring assets from one spouse to the other or dividing jointly owned property between them as part of the divorce decree.

Pro se. The legal term that describes the fact that a person involved in a court case is handling the case himself and is not represented by a lawyer.

Psychiatrist. A physician who is trained to diagnose and treat emotional and mental illness.

Psychoanalyst. A person who has undergone training in a treatment method involving long-term, in-depth probing into the patient's early childhood experiences by means of dream analysis and free association. In the United States, most psychoanalysts are physicians.

Psychological parent. That parent with whom the child has strong emotional bonds, on whom he feels dependent for his well-being and safety, and whom he would miss at a very basic level if they were separated.

Psychologist. A nonmedical specialist, usually with advanced training in psychology. Psychologists may practice clinical diagnosis and therapy and engage in counseling to help patients deal with particular symptoms or life situations. They are not authorized to prescribe drugs. Clinical psychologists are trained to administer tests designed to measure emotional maturity, intelligence, and skills and also, in some cases, to evaluate the nature and depth of relationships between children and different adults.

Respondent. See *Defendant.*

Rule to show cause. A procedure for initiating certain legal proceedings, including contempt proceedings. If the person who has been asked to come to court does not show up for the hearing, a sheriff may be sent to fetch him (a procedure called a "capeas").

Separation agreement. An agreement by the spouses, usually in writing, setting forth what they have chosen to do about custody, visitation, alimony, child support, and property division.

Shared custody. See *Alternating custody, Divided custody, Joint custody.*

Social worker. A person trained to provide support, guidance, clinical assessment, and sometimes therapy for people with nonmedical difficulties. State or city departments of social welfare that conduct evaluations to advise judges in custody cases are generally staffed by social workers.

Split custody. Usually means an arrangement in which siblings are not left together; mother and father each have custody of at least one child. See also *Divided custody.*

Uniform Child Custody Jurisdiction Act. A law designed to prevent a mother or father from asking for custody or visitation in another state if he or she does not like the custody award made by the state where the action was started.

Uniform Reciprocal Support Act. A law that allows a state to enforce another state's child support decrees.

Visitation orders. Orders specifying the right of the nocustodial parent to visit the child. They can vary from the nonspecific "reasonable visitation" (meaning that the parents are to work out the details themselves) to detailed schedules specifying which days, weeks, holidays, or birthdays the child is to spend with the noncustodial parent and how often that parent may telephone the child and the child must telephone the parent. Visitation orders, like custody, can also be interim or *pendente lite* (in effect while the divorce is pending).

Visitation rights. The court-ordered and court-enforceable right of the noncustodial parent to contact with the child. The right is not reciprocal; courts do not order the noncustodial parent to visit the child.

Suggestions for Further Reading

Bowlby, J. *Maternal Care and Mental Health.* World Health Organization Monograph Series, no. 2. Geneva: World Health Organization, 1951.

Erikson, E. *Childhood and Society.* New York: Norton, 1950.

Fassler, J. *Helping Children Cope: Mastering Stress through Books and Stories.* New York: Free Press, 1978.

Folberg, H. J., and M. N. Graham. "Joint Custody of Children Following Divorce." 12 *University of California – Davis Law Review* 522 (1979).

Fraiberg, S. *The Magic Years.* New York: Scribner's, 1959.

Freud, A. *Normality and Pathology in Childhood.* Vol. 6 of *The Writings of Anna Freud.* New York: International Universities Press, 1969.

Goldstein, J., A. Freud, and A. J. Solnit. *Beyond the Best Interests of the Child.* Rev. ed. with epilogue. New York: Free Press, 1979.

Provence, S., A. Naylor, and J. Patterson. *The Challenge of Daycare.* New Haven: Yale University Press, 1977.

Rofes, E., D. *The Kids' Book of Divorce.* New York: Random House, Vintage Books, 1982.

U.S. Department of Health, Education, and Welfare. *Day Care.* 4 vols. Washington: Government Printing Office.

Vol. 1. *A Statement of Principles.* 1970. Reprint. Office of Human Development Services, Administration for Children, Youth, and Families. 1978. DHEW publication no. (OHDS) 78–31055.

Vol. 2. *Serving Infants.* 1971. Reprint. Ed. D. Huntington, S. Provence, and R. K. Parker. Office of Human Development/Office of Child Development. 1976. DHEW publication no. (OHD) 76–31056.

Vol. 3. *Serving Preschool Children.* D. Cohen, in collaboration with A. S. Brandegee. Office of Human Development/Office of Child Development. 1974. DHEW publication no. (OHD) 74–1057.

Vol. 4. *Serving School Age Children.* Ed. D. Cohen, R. K. Parker, M. S. Host, and C. Richards. Office of Child Development. 1972. DHEW publication no. (OCD) 72–34.

Index